Dirty Goals

Dirty Goals

Breaking Conventional Rules to Achieve Your Dreams

By

ALYN KAY MITLYNG

DIRTY GOALS:

Breaking Conventional Rules to Achieve Your Dreams

About The Author

Alyn (pronounced ah-lynn) was born and raised in rural Minnesota, in the town of Montevideo. Since leaving Minnesota in 2005, Alyn has lived in South Texas, Hawaii, and currently in Lakewood, Colorado. She loves spending time enjoying the beautiful Colorado weather with her boyfriend and two dogs. *Dirty Goals: Breaking Conventional Rules to Achieve Your Dreams* is Alyn's first book.

Message to the Reader

Dear Reader,

Thank you so much for picking up this book. I believe that everyone has the ability to create happiness and fulfillment in their lives, but it is up to each one of us to figure out how. Writing this book was my journey, and it was so much fun! I hope you enjoy the book and find value in my take on goals – Dirty Goals.

Thank you,
Alyn Mitlyng

Contents

CHAPTER 1

Life Cycle According to Goals

I have always considered myself a hard worker. It's in my Minnesota genes. I know you are never supposed to say never, but I really *never* procrastinate. I like to stay busy and tend to lose focus and become overly distracted with unattended to do lists. So, when something comes across my proverbial desk, I work on it immediately. The action of crossing tasks off my list is very gratifying, and I am good at it.

Good at getting everyday tasks done. Aside from a mostly done to-do list, my house is clean, my errands are done, work is caught up, you would think that I have life figured out. Except I don't. You don't arrive at life, or ever have it all figured out. If you think you have, you are just going through the motions and are likely not growing to your full potential. We need to get out of our comfort zones. When we think we have arrived, we need to strive for more. We've only got one life, and I'm all in for knocking it out of the park. When you think you have life figured out, or that you are satisfied with what you have accomplished and are just trying to coast to the finish line, you need a different perspective and a new purpose.

The Cycle of Life

Reviewing typical milestones in the cycle of life, we live and die by goals. From very early on in life we are compared as babies and toddlers to our peers based on size, gross and fine motor skills, communication, expression, social and receptive skills at specific time intervals. Our parents work with us as babies and toddlers to influence our development to meet or exceed these development goals. As we progress into childhood people start asking what we want to be, what sports we want to play, and what our goals are when we grow up. Applying to four-year colleges sometimes requires an essay, which demonstrates your ability to work toward a goal. When interviewing for jobs we are asked about our accomplishments, where we see ourselves in 5-10 years, and how we set and achieve goals. And when we are living our elderly years, some are still setting and achieving goals, while others are sharing their life stories and accomplishments with our loved ones. Our loved ones will eventually listen to our eulogy being read highlighting our life's work. Goals have been a part of our lives from the very beginning – so why are they so difficult? Why do we so commonly stop at setting goals that align with the expected life path? I want to win the state in my sport, graduate high school, graduate college, get a good job, get married, get a promotion, get a higher degree, have kids, get a new job, get another promotion, start a new career, and eventually retire so I don't have to set goals anymore.

The purpose of this book is to challenge you to set goals that are not just the next step in life. Rather seek out goals that enhance your life with amazing experiences and fulfillment. I aim to get you to see the exponential possibilities and opportunities you are passing up every day to settle for a living in the "rat race", just to get your slice of the cheese. To motivate you to go beyond, or on a completely different path, than what anyone ever expected from you. To get your own cheese that you don't have to compete for anymore, but rather that you can create for yourself. Goals that don't just get you to where you think you should be in life, based on the expectations your world has of a life cycle. I challenge you to find goals that will change not only your life, but also others' lives for the better. Goals that take you off the beaten path and onto your own exciting, life-changing journey.

I do not have a higher degree in psychology, nor am I a life coach or an expert in setting and achieving goals. My experience with goal setting and achieving is on a personal level based on my own experience. When I realized that I had no personal goals I tried to find guidance on how to discover what my personal goals might be, but I could not find the guidance for which I was searching. There were several websites, books, YouTube videos, and podcasts on how to build goals when you have identified the end-product you want to achieve, and how to achieve goals once specific details are defined. But I could find very little direction for those of us who are struggling to find an idea for a personal goal – aka purpose.

At the time of this journey, I was a person who was going through the steps in life, letting life guide me to what was next, instead of taking the wheel and guiding my own life through setting and achieving goals. I had mistaken my career goals and successes as being enough in my life. I was on autopilot. Day by day, hour by hour, I was accomplishing tasks that got me to the achievement of work and career goals but had completely dismissed setting and achieving personal goals.

In my new quest, the only thing I was sure of was that I ultimately wanted financial freedom in the form of multiple sources of income – doesn't everybody. With no idea or details on how I would pursue this goal, I was left with a world of possibilities and very little direction with no guidance. How do I identify and then narrow opportunities to get to the action that will achieve the broad goal of financial freedom? The good news is that there are endless avenues to pursue and achieve success. The bad news is that it is your responsibility to find your avenue. The great news is that I have a method that can help you find your way.

Through the journey of finding myself and my goals, I realized that others might benefit from my story. Whether you are just starting to find your path through life, find yourself in a situation where you are having to start over, or you are successful and just need a little guidance on taking your life to the next level, this book is for you. Please don't ever think you are too old to set and achieve goals. Kurt Amplatz, an Austrian radiologist, formed a company when he was 73 years old to design a plug that treats a medical condition for holes in the septum of the heart. The company sold 13 years later for $1 Billion when he was 86 years old. You are only as old as you think you are, and as limited as you allow your mind to tell you that you are. Age really is just a number, but it is your perception of that number that sets limits.

You don't need to be seeking happiness to set and achieve personal goals. People who have already achieved peace and happiness can only elevate these feelings in the pursuit of personal goals. When you are already happy, having goals brings about an almost euphoric feeling. Just when you thought you couldn't be any happier, there you go and set personal goals that make it happen. For some reason we have this false perception that goals are meant to remedy displeasure and unhappiness with your situation and your life circumstances. Goals do offer a great opportunity to provide a distraction that will take the focus away from whatever you feel is lacking. And aside from the distraction, it naturally feels good to achieve. But you don't need to be unhappy with your circumstances to give you the motivation to set goals to initiate change. It will behoove you to understand and recognize that happiness comes from within you. Your situation and circumstances don't make you happy. The conversations you have with yourself, your perception of your life and how things should be, and your relationship with gratitude make you happy. Being happy is a decision. So decide to be happy in little moments and see how your world reacts. The outcome of your goals will likely also improve.

My hope for you is that you find a personal journey that gives you joy and fulfillment. That you learn to think outside of the box and not just focus on goals that get you to the end of the expected path through life. That you find goals throughout life that will help to make your ordinary life extraordinary. We are going to travel through your everyday thoughts and find the magic your brain has been trying to get you to see. I hope you enjoy the book, and even more, I hope you find personal success and fulfillment through putting the words on the following pages into action in your own life.

CONSIDER THIS:

Throughout the following chapters you will see these suggestions that help to enhance the experience of this book. The purpose of these exercises is to bring awareness to the power and value of a feeling or change in perspective that these sections provide. Some examples will be directly related to goals, some will be an exercise to get you to see the benefits that inducing these feelings will have on your life. You can use this realization as a motivation to improve your life and help you drive toward identifying and developing your goals. These are not just words on a page. If you treat them as that by just reading and moving on, you will not get the full benefit these sections and this book are intended to deliver.

CHAPTER 2

The Problem with Goal Setting

A Willingness to Do The Work

It is likely that in your search for fulfillment in life, you have read books such as *The Secret by Rhonda Byrne, Think and Grow Rich by Napoleon Hill, and The Power of Now by Eckhart Tolle.* You get motivated to change habits in your life and are excited as you read the book because you know your life has changed. And it has, but likely after a few days old habits reappear. Hopefully you have taken small but very valuable nuggets from those readings and adjusted some of your habits. A year or two passes and you are reminded of the book that had changed your life and think to yourself that you should reread that book, or at least a summary of the book. You felt so good when you read it. You felt reborn, like a whole new person with endless possibilities.

All of these books are amazing contributions to the personal development world and have no doubt changed many lives, mine included. These teachings have taught me that I am in control of my mental peace and happiness, and that I need to implement tools and techniques to achieve a peaceful and happy life. These thought leaders have provided tools to work through challenges in life. Like I said, amazing! But the question remains; how do we not only implement them in our everyday life, but also use them to continue to escalate our lives to the magnitude that these great writers have experienced? How do we make these changes not only incrementally, but life changing monumental transformations?

Amazing as these books are, they are only as beneficial as you allow them to be in your life. This book is no different. You feel the energy and excitement when you are reading (hopefully) but when it comes to the moment of truth and it is time to do the work –

Are you willing to put forth the effort?

Are you willing to sacrifice now to reap the benefits later?

Are you willing to overcome the fear of failure to pursue something new?

Are you willing to forget the limits of your past to believe in a limitless future?

Notice that I did not ask if you *can* put forth the effort, if you *can* sacrifice, if you *can* overcome your fear, if you *can* stop limiting yourself. You are reading this book so I already know that you *can*. Are you willing to do the work for you? For your family? For your children? The answers to these questions are completely up to you, but realize that if the answer is no – that is by choice. Unless we are willing to challenge ourselves every day, we are the self-limiting factor that hinders our lives. Don't just read these books, but do the work to implement the suggested practices that we are seeking when we choose to take the time to read them. The method I laid out in the following chapters to discover your goals does not require a ton of work in itself, and I have found the process to be a lot of fun. However, setting and achieving goals is a lot of work, so you need to be willing to commit to the process. And if you're doing it right, it will be fun and motivating and won't really feel like work at all!

Our happiness and our fulfillment is our own responsibility. The path to self-fulfillment, self-development, and overall happiness may be presented to us by authors, motivational speakers, and thought leaders, but we tend to limit our personal progress to the boundaries of our comfort zones. We are typically only willing to employ the practices we read about to some extent. The limitations of these extents are that these practices:

- Fit into the design of our lives
- Don't require too much work
- Provide immediate gratification

We are willing to work for something as long as we can experience the benefits almost simultaneously. I know this because I am also human...and also guilty of the above.

We would all do ourselves a great service to have personal expectations and constantly strive for improvement in our lives in our quest for true fulfillment. Most personal development books target adjustments in habitual behaviors to change our lives. Changing habits, no doubt, changes our lives. In this book, I propose that you consider setting and achieving personal goals to change your life entirely. Setting a goal will not only address some habitual behaviors, but will also allow you to completely change your focus to create a shift in the direction of your life. Like the books that have come before this one, the power to change your life is completely up to you. If you read this book and put it back on the shelf, that is your choice. But if you practice the suggestions provided throughout this book and continue to practice them after you finish reading, the effect on your life could be monumental. It is completely up to you.

Setting goals in our personal lives will help us to keep our focus by continually introducing a new and updated path that has the potential to keep you energized and buzzing with life. But setting goals has become this cliché thing that has become so rigid and so career focused that we often forget we are more than the single career aspect of our lives.

Why Personal Goals are Different

I like to categorize goals into 5 sub-types: Beaten path/expectation goals, career, work, resolutions, and personal goals. Most people automatically develop the first four types of goals, while the fifth type of goal belongs to the population who want to escalate their lives beyond an expectation and a paycheck and live a life of fulfillment and possibly even financial freedom. Let's explore in greater detail.

Beaten path/expectation goals. We all have expectations of ourselves as well as expectations from our parents and loved ones. Based on the achievements of our parents, siblings and extended family, there is an inherent expectation of the things we *should* achieve in life. From not only participation, but also doing well in sports (who doesn't want their child to achieve a full ride scholarship?), performing well in school (again, scholarship?), getting into a desired college, getting married to someone who fits an expected profile by a certain age in your life, producing grandchildren by a certain age, and landing the expected profile of a great job. If your parents are doctors, lawyers, or other highly educated professionals you may be expected to follow the same or similar path that ensures that you, too, are a highly educated professional. If your parents worked hard at their jobs their entire lives and think that college is a waste of time and money, you too may be expected to skip college and get straight to work. In this scenario, going to college might create resistance from your parents and siblings.

The most important thing to remember about beaten path goals is that others' expectations are someone else's goals. If you do not strive for the life and career that you are passionate about, you will struggle to live a life of joy and fulfillment. You will find yourself wishing you did something different and always wonder about the "what ifs". Family pressure can be hard to overcome but remember that you are the one who has to live with your choices on a daily basis. A 40-year career can be long and miserable if you don't enjoy the beaten path you have pursued. Examples of expectations goals include:

- A college degree, in a specific field, by a specific age
- Marriage to an acceptable partner and a specific number of children by a specific age
- A house of a specific size, in a specific location by a specific age or life milestone

Career goals. Career goals are those that grow from your beaten path or expectation goals. They are typically more self-driven and are paved with opportunities that are within your chosen career. For instance, a person who starts out as a bank teller may see other opportunities for growth within the banking industry to advance once they gain experience. The next step might be a teller line manager, personal banker, loan officer, and eventually bank president. These goals generally evolve throughout a career and are realized as opportunities become available, possibly in your current organization, possibly not. Keep in mind that managers can see your level of motivation and passion for your work, and opportunities that come available to you will be a reflection of your performance and your attitude. Just wanting your career to progress is not enough. You need to do the work to help get you there. Examples of career goals include:

- A promotion to increase responsibilities after a specific time of experience
- Specific roles you are looking for opportunities to obtain such as management or business development within a specific timeframe of your career
- Develop skills that will improve your performance in your role in a timely sequence

Work goals. Work goals help you to achieve your career goals. Perform tasks to meet your work goals well and you bump yourself up in line when career advancement opportunities come around. These goals are established in conjunction with your manager/boss and help you as an individual achieve a common goal within your organization. For instance, your company may be implementing a new computer system that you will utilize in your role. As part of the process, you may be asked to participate in testing the system, identifying issues and advantages, and then assisting in the training process for other colleagues since you have now had some experience with the system. This experience will provide you the opportunity to be the subject matter expert within your job, and give you experience in training others. These goals are generally part of your annual review and are the basis for pay increases, promotions, and sometimes bonuses. Other examples of work goals include:

- Meet a projected sales number or other metric by the end of the fiscal year, focusing on a specific product line
- Improve the process or function of your role, in a specified time, by meeting determined milestones

- Developing a program to fulfill an unmet need, at a specified time, by meeting determined milestones

Resolutions. Merriam Webster's definition of a resolution is a promise to do something different in the future. Resolutions are generally associated with the New Year and are used to achieve a desired change of routine that will have a positive effect on your life. In many cases resolutions are commitments (using this word loosely) to make better habits. A John C. Norcross study from 1988 followed 200 people who set New Year's Resolutions. 100% of the people involved in the study set New Year's resolutions – it was an inclusion criteria to be evaluated. The outcome was that 19% of people were still working on or had achieved their resolutions two years later. Of this 19% that were still working on their goals, 53% had at least one slip in their resolution. The people that were considered successful at working at these habits two years later had a mean number of 14 "slips" in the two years. A definition of "slip" would be helpful in determining if these were minor indiscretions or major failures and a reboot of the resolution. In this scenario, I argue that really 9% of the participants followed through with their resolutions. The math:

19% still working on their resolutions.

x 47% with no slips

9% true success

Even if you do not agree with my logic and math, it is clear to see how successful the general American population has in following through with resolutions to change their habits - minimal. Examples of resolutions or habit goals include:

- A detailed plan for weight loss, including specific pounds or inches, and methods to achieve weight loss
- Improved nutrition for overall health, measured in calories or macros, and included a specific nutrition plan
- Eliminate procrastination by maintaining to-do lists at specific time intervals and a specified plan for items remaining on the list

Personal goals. Personal goal setting is where the magic happens. If you have ever wanted to live a life of fulfillment that most people do not reach, personal goals are a great place to start. It has been suggested that only 3% of people have personal goals. This statistic is widely referenced and somewhat accepted as fact, even though there is no evidence that the actual study exists. I have come to the conclusion that the reason this study is so widely referenced is that very little research on goals has been collected and reported. If there is any validity to this number as a true reflection of goal setting in our society, then you can clearly see that you are already well on your way to success by the simple fact that you are reading this book and considering personal goals. You are already a cut above the majority standard. Pair the desire to set and achieve goals by writing your goals on paper, telling a family member, friend or accountability partner, and giving performance updates to that person and you have a winning equation for being a success at achieving your goals. A study completed by Gail Matthews from Dominican University found that by implementing each one of these practices, people became increasingly successful at achieving their goals.

The challenge with personal goals is that there is generally no path or expectations in which to follow. Going to college is a beaten path goal. Getting a job and accelerating your career are both part of your career and work goals. Commitments to lose weight or create better habits are resolutions to improve your quality of life and your health – commitments that you are reminded of every time you look in the mirror, go to the doctor, or realize that some function in your life is not efficient. You typically do not have family or spousal expectations in the personal goal setting category. You may even meet resistance to setting and achieving personal goals if your spouse, family, or work feels like it is distracting you from your standing commitments.

Personal goals are also the achievements we set for ourselves to make our lives more fulfilling and possibly (but not always) create an opportunity for financial freedom. Financial freedom is typically not achieved from a job, as we tend to increase our spending to match increases in income and we need to stay in our jobs to maintain our lifestyles. Saving for retirement is a common personal goal we build on throughout our careers that will carry us financially from the moment of retirement to the moment of death. But with very little wiggle room for income and spending between retirement and death, standard retirement funds do not constitute financial freedom in many cases. You might retire somewhat wealthy after investing in your 401k after 40 years of working, but that's not the kind of financial freedom we long to achieve. In order to achieve the financial freedom that will move you from collecting a paycheck to the true ability to make decisions based on what you want to do and not what you need to do to get to retirement, you need personal goals and action. Personal goals can be large changes or small adjustments that provide opportunities for fulfillment in your life. Examples of personal goals include:

- Declutter your home and your life by implementing methods that help you to be more organized and decrease stress
- Start a daily gratitude journal and write thank you notes once a month to increase awareness of all the good in your life and improve mental health
- Develop a hobby into a side business by obtaining business and technical knowledge and building a fluid business plan (more on that later)

The Hunt for Fulfillment

Most Americans live paycheck to paycheck. No matter how much money we make, we adjust our lifestyles according to the money flowing into our accounts. I am aware of a married couple, both highly paid physicians, who are in debt up to their eyeballs. They have a beautiful home and an abundance of assets that make it appear that they are living the dream. But they do not get to enjoy any of it due to the stress of finances they face on a daily basis. Their home and relationship are full of tension and anxiety brought on by the financial situation they have created. A higher paying job is not the answer to fulfillment. An abundance of assets is not the answer to fulfillment. Part of the paycheck-to-paycheck problem is that we believe "stuff" will fill this void. We see people who have big houses, nice cars, and toys and assume that their free time and lives are filled with fun and substance. When we increase our income we strive to meet a certain expectation about the things we think we should have based on the belongings and performance of our neighbors, friends and family. We also believe that everyone else is living a life of fulfillment based on their belongings. You have heard of it as "keeping up with the Jones's". Somehow, we don't learn from past experience that material things do not provide the feeling of fulfillment that is missing in so many of our lives – a feeling that will never be satisfied by what can be bought. The void can only be filled by investing time and working for yourself.

Personal goal setting is an amazing tool that can help you fill this void and discover an inner happiness. By choosing to make yourself and your mental peace a priority, you can change your situation. But most don't do the work because most don't even know that the feeling of fulfillment is a mental state – one that requires us to nurture our mind, not fill our space, to achieve.

Becoming a part of the 3 Percent

The widely referenced study that I referred to previously was reportedly done in a Harvard graduating class. The reported outcome was the 3% of students that wrote out their goals made 10 times the income compared to the other 97% combined. An additional 13% of the graduates had goals, but these goals were not written down. This 13% made twice the money of the other 84% who did not have goals. This illusive study is unfortunately not to be found in any database, however, these numbers are commonly referred to as the standard statistics for goal setting.

Three percent. Three percent of people are motivated enough to not accept mediocrity. They have figured out the secret to achieving their goals.

Or, I would argue that this three percent may have an edge because they have figured out how to determine their goals in the first place? I would like to believe we all would like to achieve the personal success of creating and achieving goals, but we get lost trying to figure out what we want to achieve. Some (probably most) of us require a little more creativity and soul searching to find our goals. With so little guidance about how to identify goals, and so much detail required to set the widely approved method of SMART (Specific, Measurable, Achievable, Relevant, and Time-based) goals, it is not surprising that the average person fails to set and achieve personal goals. In a world where our careers and responsibilities in our home lives monopolize our time and thoughts, we lose sight of the potential we have to create in our lives. Suddenly we are (or I am anyway) 43 years old and realizing that we could be achieving so much more in our everyday lives. Life has become centered on work/career goals, maintenance of family/home life, and monopolizing time commitments (unbeknownst to us) to our smartphones, social media, and television.

Do you want to focus on the good news now? By choosing to identify, develop, and achieve your goals, you are already ahead of the game. Opportunity for achievement and success is UNLIMITED! Unlimited, but hugely untapped. You are taking the first step in researching guidance for finding your goals. When you find and develop your goal, you are putting yourself in the top 13% of the population. And when you (not if, right?) work through the guidance in this book to take action in achieving your goals, you will put yourself in the top 3%. That in itself is extremely motivating.

Why do so few people set goals?

So why is the number of people who set goals so low? If setting and achieving goals improves our chances for happiness and success to such an extent, why don't more people do the work? My theory: the widely accepted SMART process to develop and achieve goals is very stuffy and limiting. We have been so engrained with the idea that the SMART goal method is a requirement, not just a guide. In business, SMART goals are necessary (we will get to that later). But for personal reasons, that just doesn't hold true. There are two main problems with this process that prevent people from setting and achieving goals.

- The process skips one of the most crucial elements in goal setting, which is to create and develop our ideas.
- We are constantly impressed upon having goals you need specific details before you can take any action.

Determining my goals was the hardest part of goal setting. I don't believe that I am alone in that challenge. Even when you have determined your goal, specific details of your goals aren't always known. Most of the time you need to take action for the details to reveal themselves. The thought that you need such detailed information to get started on taking action with your goals is crushing and demotivating. Equally as crushing to motivation (but in a "double down" fashion) is the feeling of failure associated with setting metrics that have a high probability of changing when you uncover information. In hindsight, if you leave those specifics blank and fill in the details as you gather more information, the process might turn into a motivating sequence of events. This will help you to feel like you are moving along in the process instead of having to start over, or feeling like you failed to meet your original plans.

Purpose Versus Goals

As you make your way through this process, keep in mind that when we talk about goals I am not necessarily talking about finding your "purpose", grand life meaning, or a single heroic type event that you believe you were put on earth to do. If that's your notion of goal setting, you may just be disappointed if the results fail to meet your awe-inspiring expectations. When we refer to a life purpose it leads to this grandiose connotation of epic proportions. Think of the movie *Simon Birch* – looking for his purpose in life as being a magnificent act that saved the lives of many. If your goal is to cure cancer, by all means do it! That would be an epic life purpose that will win you accolades and a guaranteed place in the history books. If your goal is to write a book or develop a product, lets achieve that goal and be proud of our accomplishment even though we are not saving a bus full of children. Curing cancer is something a person would spend a lifetime doing, therefore, that would be their life purpose. Writing a book and getting on the best seller list is relevant at this point in your life and is therefore a goal and not something that will sustain your purpose and fulfillment for an entire life.

With this in mind, I separate my "purpose" in life from my goals. I consider my "purpose" to be kind. I believe that the kindness I put out into the world may elevate one person's day, or change one person's frown to a smile. That purpose may not seem grand, but it makes me feel good every time I can have a positive effect on someone's day. I plan to keep that purpose every day because I believe it enhances my life as well as the lives of those around me. If you have a grandiose expectation of your life's purpose, you may end up living a less than fulfilled life, even though what you have done is nothing less than amazing to someone else. Recognize that small actions may have a huge impact and be okay with not knowing the full impact that your "purpose" holds.

I am going to take you along on my journey to discovering my goals and hope that it will lead you down a path to a discovery of your own. There is a good reason why our jobs require us to set goals – goals have proven to achieve success and revenue in business. If this wasn't the case, large companies would not spend the money for goal maintenance and time efforts of staff for developing, documenting, and monitoring goals. Your work goals impact the business substantially. So how much do you think goal setting would impact your personal life? I think finding out might just be worth it! Maybe my journey will be the inspiration you need to go after personal goals in your own life.

CHAPTER 3

My Personal Goal Journey

Goal Audit

I have achieved many goals in my life. It's what we do as humans. We go to work, try to improve our lives through our work and career goals. When we come home from work we consider the improvements we would like to make to our lives and our homes to which we build our expectation goals. But unless we take a look at what we are working toward, we will not know what we have made as a priority in our lives. Writing details out on paper usually clarifies the facts. I suggest you do a goal audit to reveal what you have made a priority in your life. As I audit my own goals this is what I find:

My Personal Goal Journey ///

	Expectation Goal	Work Goal	Career Goal	Resolution/ Habit Goal	Personal Goal
2 Associate's Degrees	X				
1 Bachelor's Degree	X				
1 Master's Degree	X				
An escalating career			X		
Ever changing work goals		XXX XX			
Team awards			X		
Getting (and staying) in shape				X	
Eating healthily				X	
Improve posture				X	
Buying a house	x				
Upgrade to a single family home	x				
Fixing up our home	x				
Buy a new car	x				
Build my retirement	x				

Expectation goals – check. Work goals – check, check, check (business understands how important goals are, so we are sure to always be developing these goals). Career goals – check. Resolutions – check. Personal goals – completely absent. Evaluating my beliefs based on my list of goals I have accomplished throughout my life reveals one very blatant fact; when I am feeling the need to improve my life, I have turned to expanding my education as the answer. Higher education leads to greater achievements, right? Well, kind of. More education can't hurt you, other than possibly increasing debt if you take out loans to cover the costs. Yes, I felt like I accomplished something each time I graduated. But out of all of those degrees, the only one that was truly life changing was the 2-year Associates degree in Radiologic Technology. The other bachelor's and master's degrees cover me if it is a job requirement for a job posting. That's it. So when I finished those accomplishments, it felt great. For a minute. The sequence of the feeling of achievement for both of those degrees went something like this: feeling of accomplishment, smiling, sighing, and then I think "okay, now what?"

Some of the goals we carry forward in a maintenance phase convert to habits after the goal is achieved, such as an extended exercise routine that we continue even after we reach our goal weight. Some achievements sit on a shelf getting dusty, like my two higher degrees. Between work and maintenance of daily life, why would it have even occurred to me that I was ignoring the type of goal that could have the biggest impact on my life and internal happiness? Enter *The Miracle Morning*.

CONSIDER THIS:

When I bought my first house my dad told me that you have to expect to spend at least $8,000 a year on improvements, otherwise you will end up with a money pit. Lack of goals and expectations in any category may leave you in a situation where you feel hopeless. Similar to home maintenance to avoid a catastrophe, you need to maintain your mental and physical health so you don't find yourself in a medical crisis. Strive for opportunities in your career so you don't end up burnt out and unhappy. Build on your expectation goals every day, every month, and every year so you don't find yourself at a crossroads with nowhere to turn. Take care of yourself because no one else can.

A Welcome Discovery

I love personal development books. The value of this work has helped me create a world where I am confident, motivated, accountable, and successful. When I discovered Hal Elrod's book *The Miracle Morning*, I was excited to revitalize some current practices of these valuable life tools, restart some forgotten practices, and implement some never practiced techniques. Through this *Miracle Morning* process, I was easily able to identify the aspects of my life that needed attention. There was something powerful about utilizing these tools and techniques in combination that quickly revealed the areas in which my own personal development was lacking. Know that your own road to self-discovery will be different than any other person who reads these books and practices these theories. Your personal situation is based on your unique life experiences, interests, and perceptions. I suggest this, or similar practices, to bring clarification to your own life. The specific elements that were redeeming my weaknesses may be a strength for you. In general, the weaknesses revealed to you will send you on a journey of your own.

Although I was a little disappointed with myself that I did not have any personal goals, the discovery was a welcome one. I don't recommend stewing on what you haven't done, or spending time regretting wasted time. Instead, I recommend and practice implementing positive change when discoveries such as this come to light. So I took very immediate action to remedy my situation. My journey to developing personal goals went something like this: the day I got the book *The Morning Miracle* I was super excited to start reading. The more I read, the more excited I got to start practicing all of these techniques to see where it led me. I decided that the next morning I would practice the elements of SAVERS (silence, affirmations, visualization, exercise, reading, and scribing) that I had already been practicing in my daily life from other personal development books, podcasts, and YouTube videos. I planned to wait to practice visualization and scribing since they were the items I knew less about. I knew that there were many ways to practice each of the elements of the method, so I was excited to dive in and learn something new.

The initial practice was easy. These were things I tried to do every day already, so it was nice to get them all done in the morning and not worry about making time to do them throughout the day. This is not to say that my practice of these techniques did not change. Practice gets stale and loses benefit if we don't evolve as we learn. I took suggestions from the book and did research to improve my practice on the elements I already employ. As I continued to read the chapter that laid out all of the elements including visualization and scribing, I figured adding these two new elements to my routine would be easy. I wasn't convinced they would play much in the department of benefit, but figured "I've got this"!

When morning came it was a different story. I had no idea what to visualize. What did I want? What more could I possibly want in my life other than "stuff" that I don't really want anyway (I am a moderate minimalist)? I went to the internet on my phone and typed in "how to visualize". After surfing for a while, I found a suggestion to visualize yourself after you achieve your goals. Great! I now had a little direction. But I was wrong. How do you visualize how you will feel when you achieve personal goals that don't even exist? I have goals I set for work and my career, but those are not personal. Although I love my job, I certainly hope that I am more dynamic of a person than just a single dimension of a career.

The realization that I had no personal goals really bothered me. I am a successful, hard-working, motivated woman. How could I not have personal goals? And furthermore, how could it be so difficult to try and identify one single goal that was personal? After some reflection, I determined the reasons for my lack of ability to identify goals included:

1. A lack of consideration of my own self and my desires
2. No clear passion (i.e. dreams of being a rockstar, actor, or football pro)
3. No obvious aspect of my life needing (or wanting) to change
4. The perception of little time to spend developing my person and my life as after a 40-hour work week, time at home is spent on family time, chores, and errands (and if I am being totally honest, wasted on my smart phone)
5. Not realizing the importance of goals in my personal life

Further searches on Google made another fact obvious - there is an abundance of guidance on how to set and achieve goals, but there is very little information on how to discover an idea for your goals and how to make that idea into a legitimate goal. A search on YouTube created similar results. Videos that had the right title, tons of views, and overall good ratings still did not provide the information and direction I was seeking.

I went to lay in the sun because I couldn't focus on anything else. I was so disconcerted with myself from my recent discovery. Basking in the sun lasted about 5 minutes. In those 5 minutes of intense thinking I knew I was going to write a book about how to discover personal goals. I just didn't know how to do it yet. So, I grabbed Rozi, Zoe, and Bruiser (my 3 beautiful Boston Terriers) and set out on a voyage around the park to do some thinking. Magically I found the answers I was seeking. In a matter of 4 hours I had done my first FULL Miracle Morning, discovered I had no personal goals, discovered that there was little information to help determine what my goals might be, decided to write a book, gone on a walk, and figured out how I could effectively develop my own personal goals with very little help from anything outside of my own brain. I also thought of an additional personal goal, one I am still super excited about but is purposefully delayed.

I have always heard that when things are meant to happen, you will be provided with the information to make it possible. I took the momentum I had created that morning and used it to continue my journey by starting this book THAT DAY! My brain was in high gear and I knew that God and the universe had provided me with a challenge that roused excitement in me and is now allowing me to share it with others.

Dirty Motivation

Before my journey I would never have related having personal goals as being an accelerator for career efficiency and drive. I have always labeled myself as a hard worker and have always stood by my values and ethics. I was (in many aspects – but not all) an easy person to manage because I got the work done in a complete and efficient manner, and always followed the rules. When I set personal goals, everything was enhanced for the better. I was so much more focused, so much more efficient, and so much more valuable in my role at work. I wasn't only creating ideas for my personal goals, I found myself using the same technique and asking questions to create opportunities at work as well. Essentially, the motivation I got from setting goals bled into and increased the motivation I had at work. I ended up with extra projects at my already busy job, but I was so motivated that I became more efficient and fit more tasks into less time. I structured my days to make sure that I was devoting time for my own goals in the morning and evening, and focusing only on work tasks during business hours. Previously my workday would bleed into the mornings and evenings, but with this new-found excitement and drive, my workdays became so focused that I could fit my old tasks and my new opportunities all within regular business hours.

Having experienced the effect personal goal setting had on multiple aspects of my life, I believe that people who pursue goals outside of work become more successful and valuable in their careers. I know I was exponentially more motivated, creative, and efficient. I believe this effect is likely in anyone who actively pursues their ideas to create goals.

Some great things can come out of discovering your personal goals. But, as I stated before, it is completely up to you to move beyond a theory or words in a book. It is up to you to implement personal goal setting in your life. Before we get started on the process, let's understand the premise behind the theory of dirty goals and tackle all of those pesky reasons people talk themselves out of goal setting.

CHAPTER 4

The Dirty Concept

Why Would I Create Dirty Goals?

Early in my journey to writing this book I was working out on my favorite exercise program, *21 Day Fix with Autumn Calabrese*. As you will see through this journey, one of the best times to collect your thoughts is when you are working out. As you are aware of and actively observing your thoughts, you recognize when something significant passes through your mind. My favorite workout in the program is the Dirty 30. My sister and I have both been doing this workout for several years, so that particular morning I was reminiscing on a conversation we had one day about why it is called the Dirty 30.

I have never tried to google the answer, but what we came up with was that the workout is about 30 minutes (hence the 30), and you break the conventional rules of strength training (chest and tricep day, leg day, back and bicep day, and so on) by combining (hence the term dirty) multiple exercises to incorporate multiple muscles at the same time, which increases your heartrate to incorporate cardio as well. The benefit of this method is that you work multiple muscle groups in less time while burning more calories. Wins all around!

While considering the method behind the Dirty 30 I suddenly realized that the method I had uncovered to identify and develop goals was very similar. Instead of following the conventional and accepted method to brainstorm ideas, define the specific metrics of that idea to develop a goal, and only then begin taking action, they had been smushed together to make the process more efficient, more motivating, and easier to define the specifics along the way. Like the workout, my method of determining and setting goals was also dirty.

Although I loved the name Dirty Goals, I did have a little hesitation due to the negative connotation that comes along with the word. When you look up the meaning of dirty on Merriam-Webster you will find the following definition:

Not clean or pure
Morally unclean or corrupt
Abominable, hateful
Not clear or bright
Deceptive
Soiled

So why would you ever want to read a book about setting dirty goals? I challenge you to consider dirty in a good way, as there are many ways this word is used in a positive reference. Consider the following:

1. The phrase "get your hands dirty", which means to dig in and get involved, and to do the hard work - whether it involves mud or not.
2. Dirty rice – it's just rice with a whole lot of delicious extras added (yum!).
3. Dirty but healthy bacteria nutrition professionals and doctors tell us to eat in the form of probiotics to promote gut health.

4. Quick and Dirty Tips (QDT)– A website educating on a better way to do things from a variety of professionals in the areas of fitness, money, parenthood, science, nutrition, psychology, relationships and household tips. Quick and Dirty Tips ™

5. Conventional thinking about cleaning our home and making our beds can be the dirtier option? It has been discovered that making your bed every morning provides a cool damp place for mites to feast on your skin particles throughout the day - yuck.

6. I can't leave out the "Dirty 30" workout, which alters the conventional thinking of strength training by working multiple muscle groups at one time to burn more calories, in less time, making "dirty" more efficient.

   And I can't really stop without talking about the amazing work of the core word "dirt".

7. Dirt – a necessary ingredient and one of the 3 (air and water being the other two) requirements of life for all of the beautiful plants and trees on earth. Dirt provides the required nutrients and stability to provide the food we eat every day.

Dirty doesn't always have to suggest the negative. Dirt is the support under our feet, the home where our food is grown and the method to make life more efficient. All the amazing goodness that comes out of the dirty concept is an amazing way to approach life in your own way.

The term dirty, in the sense of this book means that you take a topic, such as goals, and you bend the rules of conventional thinking to be able to approach the issue from a different angle and make it more efficient for you. Your thoughts and actions are the dirt from which great ideas develop into beautiful goals. In order to be successful in the dirty concept, you need to recognize that just because a certain task has been done in a specific way in the past, doesn't necessarily make it "right" or the only way.

I do the work the way I want to do the work. Not the way someone tells me to do the work. It is how I approach pretty much everything in life. Rules are meant to be broken and methods are meant to be shaped to fit into your individual life. Make the goals you want to reach - be it physical, mental, personal, career, or work – and bend, flex, and shape them to work with your life. There are a million ways to do any task. Don't be discouraged by the rules.

CONSIDER THIS:

Someone with an A type personality may have difficulty with this method, as these people tend to strive for perfection. But who decides what is perfect? The way you have been told to do something specific is not the "right" way, but the way that works for someone else. Don't let someone else decide how you are going live your life. You drive that bus. Choosing not to participate or pursue an endeavor entirely because a specific method doesn't work for you is self-defeating and lacks imagination. Change your life by changing your methods. You were not made from a cookie cutter, so stop living like it.

What's the Problem with Current Methods?

There are multiple benefits to methods of goal setting and achieving, such as the widely used method of SMART goals. I absolutely see the value in these methods of goal setting. The benefits of these concise methods are that they provide:

- Accountability
- Focus
- Clarity
- Motivation

The caveat to the above is that this is the same list that would describe the cons of setting SMART goals. When trying to follow the SMART goals reference, the lack of wiggle room makes the whole process very unmotivating. How can you be accountable for details that you lack experience in and haven't even taken action to learn? How do you focus on the details of SMART goals before you take action to figure out the details? How do you gain clarity without taking action? And how do you get motivated if you can't take action before you have details? The result would be staring at a piece of paper racking your brain for answers you don't have the resources to determine.

The SMART goal method works well for goals that you have the experience to support the answers. For instance, if someone is setting a resolution to lose weight, you already know what actions you can specifically take to achieve your goal, what metrics you will use to evaluate your progress, and you know that weight loss is achievable at a reasonable number and timeframe. Being healthy is always relevant but rather an issue of awareness and avoidance. Setting a timeframe to achieve this goal can be easily estimated based on the accepted standard of 1 lb per week as a suggested healthy weight loss guidance by the health and medical industries. The results of this weight loss goal would look something like this:

> **S** – I am going to lose weight by walking 3 miles every day and eliminating snacks between meals.
> **M** – 10 pounds
> **A** – Yes, I have done it before.
> **R** – My clothes are no longer fitting and I feel out of breath quicker than I have in the past.
> **T** – 10 weeks

As a reminder, SMART is Specific, Measurable, Achievable, Realistic, and Timely. This same principle typically applies well to work goals. Even if you have not performed a task or worked on a specific goal before, your manager or someone establishing the business goal has and provides the guidance to set goals that meet required parameters. The key to setting SMART goals is experience and/or guidance on expectations. Without either of these, setting SMART goals is unrealistic in itself.

Personal goals are different because there is a very good chance that your thoughts that have become goal ideas are areas that you have not traveled previously. That makes defining these personal goal specifics more difficult due to lack of familiarity. Take the goal I am currently procrastinating on as an example. I have never worked anywhere in the bedding business before, nor have I ever started my own business, worked on a prototype, or had to deal with state laws for sales tax identification numbers. In all honesty, the fact that I needed a sales tax ID number to purchase wholesale material added a task to my plate of which I was completely unaware. The addition of this task came up abruptly and would inevitably affect my time metric.

The only detail I can honestly answer is that the addition of this task will not be the last surprise. This is all extremely new to me, so I am developing these ideas as I move along in the process. I am not going to stop taking action to move toward my goal just because there are so many unknowns. It was during the process of taking action that I uncovered this information very early in my journey. The ultimate purpose of dirty goals is to have a process that helps you develop your thoughts and ideas and give them room to expand, while allowing the specific details to reveal themselves through taking action.

Every method that has been created, no matter how widely used, does not work for everyone nor every situation. And every method out there - no matter how widely accepted - is waiting for a better, more evolved method to come along. In a business sense, SMART goals work and they provide a detailed plan that allows a team to follow. SMART goals also allow managers/bosses to ensure the team is working toward a common goal that is driven by overall company goals. But that doesn't mean that it is the only method for developing business goals, or the best method for creating personal goals. If there is something you want in your personal life, figure out what it is and do the work to figure out how to get there. This book might be the catalyst you need to help you do just that.

Are you on board with dirtying up your personal goals? Do you think you can fit goals into your life if they don't take over your life? In the next chapter we will tackle some of the ways we sabotage ourselves when it comes to personal goals. Let's put the kibosh on the negative resistance before we even encounter it so we can get to the rewarding work.

CHAPTER 5

Self-Sabotage

Goal setting and achieving can be a challenging task from beginning to end. Identifying goals was a challenge for me until I figured out a method to TAP into my thoughts. Setting goals is probably the easiest part of the process because it only requires a statement that you will achieve a specific action – with or without specific details. The follow-through of action and achieving goals – well that's another story. An article printed by Forbes suggests that only 8% of people achieve New Year's resolutions. I argue that most didn't fail to achieve their goal, they just decided it was not worth the effort required to meet their resolution. Their failure was a failure to try.

There are a multitude of reasons we fail or give up on our goals. From self-sabotage and self-limitation, setting our intentions on the rewards instead of actions, competing with others instead of challenging ourselves to grow, and forcing results that are not yet realized. This is not an all-inclusive list, but it is a good place to start to identify - and work to eliminate - these behaviors in your journey. Below each of the self-limiting factors are discussed and accompanied by realities that counter your negative and self-defeating thought processes. These reality statements are meant to help you change your view and combat these negative thoughts. Think about them, let them sink in and when you catch yourself wallowing in negative thoughts, remember the alternative and let yourself erase these hindering perceptions.

Other's Opinions

We are our own worst critics, and our own worst saboteurs. Our insecurities lead us to believe that others think these same critical thoughts of us. The sooner you realize that you are not the center of anyone's universe but your own, the sooner you can get to living. Anthony DeMello's book *Awareness* is a great book to read if you struggle with this concept. Somehow, we think that people care so much about what we are doing that we become consumed with it, and somehow we think others thrive off of our failures. Take a step back and think about the reality of this flawed thinking: is there any other person you put as much time and energy criticizing than yourself? I guarantee you there is not. Honestly, our criticism of others is fleeting at best. The criticisms that do come from others are usually a reflection of their own insecurities. I feel confident in promising you that other people are consumed with their own lives and their own self-doubt. The people that we do think about more than others are the ones we love, cheer for, and wish only success.

REALITY CHECK:

Imposter Syndrome is one unfortunate example of this phenomenon. From my perspective, imposter syndrome is the mental struggle that comes along with the theory of "fake it until you make it". If you struggle with the idea that you lack the skills, knowledge, and ability to do your job or are underserved of your achievements, consider a different narrative to your story. We are all learning our jobs, new skills, and processing information constantly. When people stop learning and stop trying to achieve something that is thought to be out of their skillset, we get bored. You don't grow and learn by sticking to what you have already achieved. You are not an imposter. Unless you have blatantly lied about your qualifications, you are simply out of

your comfort zone, which is where growth happens.
Good for you!

If you are on social media, you have surely seen the meme that says "Keep winning in private. Not everyone needs to know what they are up to." Everyone has an opinion. Everyone. There is a chance that someone's negative opinion can throw you off or make you lose excitement for your goals. It is unfortunate that we are willing to give that much value to another person's unsubstantiated opinion. Especially since there are people who make trolling social media to criticize others their one and only hobby. Are you going to let someone bring you down who is clearly so dissatisfied with life that they find every opportunity to bring hate to people they don't know about scenarios to which they have no insight? If you let them get to you, they win. To avoid being sidetracked by opinions of others, just get to work on your goals. If you want to tell someone, tell someone who will likely support you and who will help to keep you on track for your goals (more on this later). If you want to live your life on a level most do not experience, you can't let the opinions of others influence your road to success. As a general rule, plan to keep your goals mostly to yourself, so that you may not be influenced by the mediocrity of others.

REALITY CHECK:

Most people who criticize or demean others have a habit of that behavior. It's so easy to get discouraged by negative people and comments. In reality, these people tend to be critical of most things. To validate this as fact, I have a funny (kind of cynical) exercise I do if I run across a negative review on any review platform. When I see an extremely negative review that criticizes everything about an establishment, I click on the person who left the review to see what other reviews they have taken the time to share. You won't be surprised to know that when someone is exceptionally critical in one review, their other reviews are rarely positive and are also usually very sharp in nature. A reasonably happy person leaving a negative review will be fair and not typically harsh. Do not let these people stop you from working toward your personal goals (or stop you from visiting these establishments they have targeted). If you do, their negativity wins. Keep in mind that I do not do this exercise often, because it's better practice to avoid bringing others unhappiness into your life – God forbid it would rub off!

Self-Limiting Thinking

Our abilities are only limited to our thoughts. If we believe that something is not possible then we are acting in a self-limiting nature. As long as we hold onto these beliefs, we decrease our opportunities to succeed beyond our own imaginations and expectations. The following actions will help in your efforts to change this belief:

- **Cut the negative self-talk.**
  The first step in changing these beliefs is to recognize the negative "I can't" thought pattern when it is happening. Our goal is to stop automatically considering the impossibilities. Don't even give thoughts of impossibilities a platform.

- **How can you make your idea possible?**
  Now, ask yourself *how* this scenario could be possible. If you don't automatically have the answer, give yourself time to search your thoughts for ideas, search the internet, or ask for input from others who may have ideas to share.

- **Educate yourself**
  Learn the skills to make the task possible or take baby steps in working to understand the options and opportunities to make a goal realistic.

Don't dismiss an idea just because you don't think it is in your wheelhouse. Skills are meant to be learned. A goal I have saved for the future is developing the skills to do some home renovations. I am so inspired by people who can do amazing projects in their home with their own hands. I love that they have the vision to create and see not only the possibilities, but also make spaces multi-functional. This creativity and ability to visualize does not come easily to me. My first step will be changing the narrative in my head in regard to my capabilities. I have always told myself (and everyone else) that I can't even buy a throw pillow that will look good in a space – this narrative needs to change. My second step will be to pursue classes that will teach me the skills I need to make it happen. I am so excited and inspired that I know someday I will – but that someday is not today. Writing is my goal today – and I know this is exactly what I am supposed to be doing. I have all the confirmation I need that I am on the right path because I am having fun in the process and the ideas are coming to me freely and easily. Through the process discussed in this book, you will learn how to stop reasoning all the impossibilities and figure out the unlimited possibilities of altering a goal or idea to make it a reality.

REALITY CHECK:

When trying to reason with yourself about your limits, realize that a big reason for your doubt is because you haven't tried this same task before. If it's something you want to do, research and learn the skills. In today's world you can take classes to learn any skill, either online or in person. We are running out of excuses to be self-limiting.

Mistaking Fantasies for Goals

I want a 40-foot yacht. Doesn't everybody! But having a goal of attaining material property is not a goal in itself. Without measurable and actionable details, achieving a yacht is considered a dream or fantasy. Having dreams and fantasies about the things we would like to have in our life – be it tangible assets or situational circumstances – feels good. It feels good to picture yourself on a yacht or with your ideal partner. You are not going to achieve either of those things sitting on your couch playing video games or with your nose buried in your phone (well unless you get creative, but that takes action). Dreams and fantasies do have benefits as they allow us to escape, understand our goals and desires, and/or get motivated. But if you want to translate those feelings into real life scenarios, you need to take action and develop a plan to get you there.

REALITY CHECK:

Fantasies do have positive aspects in our lives as discussed above. Recognize that although fantasies seem like a place we would all love to live, they lack the challenges and struggles that help us to grow, learn, and become better versions of ourselves. I know a life without struggle might sound awesome, but without struggle life would lack fulfillment. Embrace your struggles and use them to show yourself - and the world - just how strong you are!

Competition

Competition is good for the soul – a quote I will never forget from a childhood favorite movie, *Girls Just Wanna Have Fun*. There is nothing wrong with competition as long as we keep it where it belongs. If you feel like you are constantly competing with others to get to where you are going, you are not living your dreams or your life. Constantly striving for goals that can only belong to one person teaches you to live on guard. The only achievement here is the walls you are constantly building so no one sees and steals your strategy to take away your top position. Living to win at everything does not provide purpose or fulfillment. There is enough success in this world to go around...for everyone. Stop focusing on goals where there can only be one winner. Create goals that you can win at and no one else has to come in second for you to feel accomplished. Create your own success on your own terms. Success is limitless, but not if you're always competing for it. Get to know yourself. Get creative. Strive for your own goals and success. Someone else does not have to lose for you to win.

REALITY CHECK:

It is commonly referred to as the concept of the rat race. This concept applies to a single piece of cheese that only the top rat gets to enjoy. Win the rat race, win the cheese. Be one of many that are up for a promotion, but only the chosen rat gets to enjoy the cheese. The basic concept applies to competition within our careers. Get out of the rat race and win at life. Win at setting your own path and achieving something more than a competition. The fulfillment of creating your own success will last longer than the piece of cheese.

Forcing the Wrong Goals

Goals are supposed to be fun and inherently motivating because the purpose of our goals are relevant to our lives. When goals are forced they become daunting tasks and are highly likely to fizzle out before they are achieved. If you achieve a goal that is forced, the achievement will not bring you the satisfaction in which goals are meant to deliver.

Reasons we find ourselves forcing our goals include trying to live up to someone else's expectations and setting goals or expectations for which you are not passionate just for the purpose of having a goal. Both of these scenarios leave you with goals that lack passion, which inhibits our creativity and drive to reach our goals with heart. Living someone else's goals is the equivalent of competition, without the edge of passion. A passion to win is motivation enough for many people to get to the finish line, but without passion where does the motivation for creativity and a desire to finish originate? Passion and excitement for your goals is what allows you to be creative and achieve great successes. Consider your passion and creativity for your goals as your signature or your personal touch. Without your signature, all you have created is a printed version of your goal that someone without a heart has the potential to achieve. Develop your own goals that are relevant to your life and that you are excited about, and be proud of the signature you put on your achievements.

REALITY CHECK:

If everything about a goal is challenging, you may want to take steps to either find a new goal or adjust the goal to fit the relevance in your life (i.e. get a new perspective on your goal). If you are working on a relevant goal at a relevant time in your life, the universe will provide the tools and information to help you achieve your goal.

Blame

Blame. What a colossal waste of time. One of my absolute favorite books of all time, *The Secret Law of Attraction* by Craig Beck, first brought my awareness to the behavior. I never gave much attention or thought to the use or effect of blame in my life. I couldn't tell you how much it was present in my life before I listened to his audio book (three times, because it is THAT GOOD). I can tell you that this tactic has no benefit to any person involved. Blame solves nothing, wastes everybody's time, and leaves all parties to walk away feeling bad about the situation. Blame provides excuses that give other people power and control over our circumstances. In the case of any type of goal setting, it provides excuses for not setting goals, not achieving goals, and ultimately choosing to let others' actions keep you from achieving your goals. There will always be resistance, but it is the obstacles that you overcome that make achieving goals so amazingly rewarding. Stop creating obstacles by using others' actions and choices as an excuse to be mediocre. Achieving a goal is not nearly as rewarding if the process is easy. Goals without challenge are not motivating, and ultimately a goal cannot exist without the presence of challenge. Let's agree that you are not going to let what has held you down in the past hold you down moving forward. The focus going forward will be on your amazing ability to overcome and succeed.

"A man may fall many times, but he won't be a failure until he says someone pushed him"
– ELMER G. LETTERMAN

REALITY CHECK:

Blaming others gives them control over your life. Others' actions may have hurt you in the past, but don't let them have control over your entire future. Forgive them, forget the damage they have done to your life and get to being great for yourself.

Fear of Failure

Fear of failure is a tough element to overcome. Failure are the opportunities in life that build us into strong, smart, experienced and adaptable human beings. So why are we so afraid of failure? We have this belief that our fear of failure helps us to avoid embarrassment and keeps us safe. We are hesitant to try something new for fear that we won't be good at that something. I am not sure where along the line we started to believe that we would rather do nothing than do it poorly the first time. Growing up, teachers taught us lessons and we studied until we were prepared to take the test. Coaches provide feedback and guide us on improvement in sports in practice, and we get to show our skills and improvements from game to game. When we were teenagers in school, learning and practicing and getting better was what we did.

Somehow, after graduation, we settled for not trying in the high probability we will need improvement. Becoming an adult does not come with an expectation that you are good at everything you will try. The fact is, the only way we fail is to stop trying.

Fear of failure also supports our decisions to take the safe route. The career we are in provides a stable paycheck. The work we do is familiar and real – not just an idea that may not pan out. The habits we perform every day have a known outcome where we don't have to admit that we tried something new and failed. Safe. And boring. Can we change our perspective? Can we consider that mediocrity of settling for our everyday habits just eat away at our time and bring us the same outcome as the day before, and the day before yesterday. Try something different for a different outcome – you might like the results. If you don't like the results, the lessons from that failure can be just as enlightening.

A project done by Adam McCaffrey at Carleton University in Ottawa, Canada, revealed that higher levels of fear of failure predict higher procrastination. However, when a level of competence within a goal exists, procrastination decreases, which in turn increases your chance for success. The lesson out of this information is both relevance and skill. In setting personal goals, consider your level of knowledge, experience, and relevance to your life thus far. If you have never bought or sold real estate, remodeled a home, or have an understanding of basic maintenance, the goal of starting a fixed and flipped business might not happen tomorrow, if at all for you. However, if you set a goal of learning the business from these different perspectives, or find the resources to fill in where you lack knowledge and skill, your chances of being successful and not procrastinating on your goal are likely to increase exponentially. If you have a big goal that you don't know much about, do the work to increase your competence. One way to navigate this phenomenon is to make your goals small to learn the business, and if those goals ignite a spark in you, then go big! But don't procrastinate to get started – take action while the spark is still burning.

If my words about failure are not convincing enough, consider the lessons from some amazingly successful and intelligent people who have known both failure and success:

"Failing to fail makes you a failure"
– ALBERT EINSTEIN

"Failure is not the opposite of success, it's part of success"
– ARIANNA HUFFINGTON

"Many of life's failures are people who did not realize how close they were to success when they gave up"
– THOMAS EDISON

"Success consists of going from failure to failure without loss of enthusiasm"
– WINSTON CHURCHILL

"Everything you want is on the other side of fear"
– JACK CANFIELD

"Our greatest glory is, not in never failing, but in rising every time we fall"
– OLIVER GOLDSMITH

"Only those who dare to fail greatly can ever achieve greatly"
– ROBERT F. KENNEDY

"There are no failures – just experiences and your reactions to them"
– TOM KRAUSE

"I have not failed. I've just found 10,000 ways that won't work"
– THOMAS EDISON

REALITY CHECK:

Failure is a choice to stop pursuing an idea or activity because you hit resistance. A CHOICE. You only fail if you stop the pursuit. If you find a way to overcome the challenge and meet your goal, you will eventually succeed.

Excuses

I am going to guess that you are really busy. You truly feel like you don't have enough time in your day already, much less to incorporate personal goals into your life. I get it. You work all day, and you look forward to unwinding at the end of the day. You look forward to the reward of relaxation to watch television or have phone time.

We are all busy. We all have homes, significant others, friends, kids, pets, parents, chores, errands, and a million other little things sucking up our time. I want you to release the thought of your busy schedule and your commitments for just a moment. Now that you don't have a constant scroll of your to-do list flashing behind your eyeballs, I want you to ask yourself the following questions:

How much time have I spent on my phone today? I am willing to bet that you are going to say somewhere around the hour mark. Fortunately (or maybe unfortunately) there is this great function on all smartphones that keeps track of the time you spend on your phone overall. It also has this fancy ability to break down the overall time to time spent on specific apps and web pages. If you are listening to podcasts or reading books from your phone, good for you. These tasks will substantially increase your phone screen time. But I ask that you be honest with yourself about the time spent on social media apps. Look at the time you spend on each of those platforms to bring awareness around where you are spending your time. If you are spending an hour on each of your social media platforms, that time spent could be of better use. I highly suggest the Netflix documentary "The Social Dilemma" to anyone that is on social media to any extent. I also suggest you have a serious conversation with yourself about how you feel after you get off your social media accounts. A while back I quit Facebook because I always felt crummy when I got done browsing the platform, I never felt happy or uplifted. I also realize that I would keep scrolling for something to pique my interest – but we keep scrolling to be disappointed with repeat posts and information that isn't really that interesting. It is so easy to get stuck. Stop the cycle. Fill that time with something that will fulfill you, not drain you.

Am I binge watching Netflix? I love me some Netflix! Especially the latest Nate Bargatze comedy special – his comedy is clean and hilarious. Watching television in the many forms that are now available is a good escape...in moderation. Maybe every night for a half hour, or even an hour. However, binge watching 8 hours of *Breaking Bad* on a Saturday afternoon? Suddenly the "I don't have time" argument has no validity. I am going to suggest a different perspective on binge watching tv. The perspective that these relaxing end-of-day rituals are draining you more than your busy day. Sitting on your phone or vegging out in front of the television for endless hours steals from your day and gives nothing back to you.

Working on personal goals has the opposite effect. When I started setting goals I found I had so much more energy, I was happier, more helpful to those around me, more present in the time with my loved ones and I had so much more excitement for life. It seemed like time multiplied because my time wasn't wasted.

The ONLY person that the "I'm too busy" excuse affects is you – the person who makes the excuse. If you want to watch tv, then watch tv. If you want to be extraordinary and set personal goals to become successful, then do that instead. YOU are the person that the choice affects. But be honest with yourself about your choice. YOU are choosing to spend your time one way or another. Stop making excuses and at the very least be honest with yourself.

REALITY CHECK:

You prayed for a cake. God provided flour, eggs, oil, icing, a pan, and an oven, you get frustrated and leave the kitchen. -Author unknown via Autumn Calabrese

If you don't do the work to develop and achieve your goals, but rather are given the end result, how do you expect to be rewarded with the feeling of fulfillment that comes with YOU ACHIEVING your goals? Quit making excuses and do the work – the reward at the end is worth it. Make the decision today to be great today!

Waiting For the Right Time

One of the biggest mistakes we make in life is to assume that "I will be happy when...". Right along these same lines, we tell ourselves that we will set goals when the timing is right. When I am less busy at work, when the kids graduate, and when things settle down in life. I was on a call with my writing coach and he shared his observation that the people who are busy in other aspects of their lives are the ones who are taking action to write books. It is not the people who have time to write books that are achieving the goal. The behavior that sets these people apart is that they no longer said they were going to wait until all of the stars aligned, they decided to take action and make their goals work in their lives right now. We have all heard the cliché that we are only promised today. Cliché or not, it is true. The only way to make our lives better tomorrow is to act today. We will always have other things that are consuming our time. Make the decision to prioritize you and your happiness and choose today.

REALITY CHECK:

Kids and family are a very common reason parents have "no time". I won't throw stones because I do not have kids, and I do appreciate the demands parents face every day. However, I think that kids are the biggest reason to find the time to set goals. Your kids will learn from watching you. If you live a life of setting and achieving personal goals, your kids will have a role model to set them up for awesome success. Squeeze in time on your lunch break, while waiting on your kids, or find a personal goal that your family can participate in and help you achieve. Be creative. You will thank yourself when your kids emulate the behavior.

The issues discussed in this chapter are not the exception. They are common behaviors that limit our true potential. Recognizing these limiting behaviors allows you to take measures to remove them from your life and achieve more than you ever imagined. These limiting behaviors are ultimately all excuses. Excuses that affect you (and your family) more than anyone else. When you vocalize excuses, you are doing it for your own justification while everyone else is stuck listening to it. You might think that is a harsh statement, but it is true. You will serve yourself better to live on autopilot and save everyone the energy and time of having to listen to your excuses. Take the time to really consider and stop these limiting behaviors. There are a million reasons not to change, not try, and settle for the lives we are living on autopilot. In the altered words of Lady Gaga, we can all think of a million reasons not to, we just need one good reason to do the work – that reason is us. The reason is our families and the people we love.

Now that we have gotten the bitter truth out of the way, let's move on and put those excuses behind us. In the following chapter we will discuss the generally accepted method of goal setting and ways we can dirty up that method to make it work in your life.

CHAPTER 6

Abolishing Old Beliefs

Goal setting? Goal setting is what is required at my job. Goal setting was for getting through college and making changes to improve my life. But things are good now, so I shouldn't have to set personal goals anymore, right? I had long left personal goal setting in the past, thinking that having good habits, a job I love, and a happy life negated the value of goal setting. I have evolved into believing that the purpose of goal setting was two-fold:

1. To get everyone on the same page to work towards the same target
2. Make changes in your life because you are not happy with the way things are

The above assumption is not necessarily wrong, but it is short-sighted. Yes - if you are struggling to change a relationship, a job that is not fulfilling, a habit that you would like to ditch, or working with others to achieve a common goal, then goal setting is a tool you will want to utilize. In my situation, I was feeling successful in a great relationship, a job that I love, healthy workout and nutritional habits (okay, the nutrition part could use some help), financial stability, and most importantly I was happy. I was floating through the motions of life not realizing that my lack of personal goals was keeping me from realizing a heightened and intensified feeling of fulfillment and excitement.

When faced with the reality that I had no personal goals, I tried to identify a goal that would be motivating and exciting for me to achieve. Instead, I immediately felt overwhelmed and confused. I couldn't understand how I had felt happy and fulfilled for so long, but this realization had suddenly made me feel disappointed that I had let my life roll on autopilot. Whether the above scenario is your story, you feel like you haven't yet found success or fulfillment, or anywhere on the spectrum in between, personal goal setting is for you!

General Accepted Goal Setting Process

Setting any type of goal is very common, but the follow-through to achievement of goals – especially personal and resolution goals - is very low. There are industries (i.e. life coaching) and methods (i.e. SMART) designed to help guide your journey toward success. The generally accepted road to the goal setting process looks something like this:

1. Brainstorm to identify your goals

2. Create SMART goals

3. Write down your SMART goals

4. Create an action plan

   a. Timelines

   b. Next logical steps

5. Take action

6. Re-evaluate and assess

The SMART method is the most utilized method in which we are taught to set and achieve goals. The what, why, when, where and how of goal setting. In the initial journey to discovering my goals, I did not have enough information to build out any of these elements with any confidence. And if I am being completely honest, my goals have become SMART without me really acknowledging the SMART principle (I know, I know – I'm out here just willy-nilly achieving goals). To develop my goals I had to start with recognizing the value of my own thoughts and ideas. This discovery is an outcome of my own mental data mining, as multiple internet search results did not provide the general guidance I was seeking on how to discover personal goals. Maybe my choice of words for searching was insufficient, as the magic words for a specific result on the internet are not always easy to produce. Either way, the guidance was difficult to locate.

The SMART goal process is a great strategy for the 1% (one of the 80% of statistics that are made up on the spot) that have a personal goal in which the elements or desired end-result are already clear. These people have a passion or purpose that they have already had time to iron through the details to apply to the SMART goal principle. The process laid out in the book has already been achieved by their own means, because identifying their goal was something that had already occurred to them.

An Alternative Way of Thinking

SMART goals work. If they didn't, experts and business wouldn't be utilizing the process. However, I suggest that SMART goals are not the only way to develop and achieve goals, and might not be the best avenue when considering personal goals. Consider an alternative and compare:

Specific

SMART:	Well defined and clear.
DIRTY:	An evolving idea that changes with information, knowledge, and experience.

Measurable

SMART:	Specific measurable criteria. (metrics by which goal progression will be evaluated)
DIRTY:	Determine metrics as these details become apparent. In this scenario, the

progression to your goals can be measured and evaluated by the accomplishment of meeting time commitments you set to develop your goals. Give yourself credit for meeting the daily or weekly time commitments you set to work toward your goals.

Achievable

SMART: Attainable, not impossible to achieve.

DIRTY: If you can dream it, you can achieve it. It may not look like the original idea upon completion, but through the process of TAPping (see chapter 9) into your goals your ideas will evolve into something amazing and achievable.

Realistic

SMART: Realistic and relevant to your life's purpose.

DIRTY: Again, you are only limited to your imagination. If you can think about it, you can work through the process of making the idea realistic. And chances are, if your mind is thinking about it, it is likely relevant to your life at this point. Get creative and don't let anyone put you in a box.

Time-based

SMART: Clearly defined timeline with target completion date.

DIRTY: Desired timeline that is flexible to be moved up or down according to information and resources gained. Set flexible end date, and stick with your time commitments during the week to work on your goals. But don't let a delayed timeline be a motivation killer.

Do you see a theme? I want you to stay committed to your goals and your person because you are worth the effort. When you set time commitments to work on your goals, stick with the commitment of a specific amount of time, but be flexible about varying times of day. If you have the opportunity to participate in a fun family day, take it! Adjust and commit to making up that time to work toward your personal goals later in the day or the next day. Commit to your goals, but don't get bogged down by the specifics. Know that without a doubt life will challenge your schedule and other priorities may steal your time. Let it happen, don't stress about it, and be present with whatever requires your time, at the time.

Through the Dirty Goal process, the information obtained and the adjustments made to your goals may cause there to be very little resemblance to the details you had when you started out. When our goals change because we have gained information that does not support the original plan, it's common to think that we have failed to meet our goal. This may contribute to a loss of motivation because details are not working out like we had planned. Changes and evolution *are* the plan for Dirty Goals. I like to think of goals as always being a rough draft. They are subject to change at any time based on knowledge acquired. I dare you to consider that changes in the specifics of your goals are a good thing. These changes mean that you are making progress. You and your goals are evolving, and you are closer to a realistic and achievable end result.

Room To Grow

I believe a major player in the reason people don't set more goals is because we are all tied to a SMART - or similar – goal process that is stuffy and doesn't leave room for our ideas to grow into goals. A significant number of people don't have the information to follow this generally accepted plan, so instead, most of us don't even bother.

Using the alternative (Dirty) way of thinking described in the last section, I suggest that we dirty up the generally accepted goal setting process. Let's mix up our trained way of thinking to gain a new perspective on goal setting. A whole new way to set goals that leave room for ideas to blossom before we get to all the details. This is a new way to look at goals as opportunities to work toward rather than something rigid and specific that takes away from the excitement of working through our goals. I suggest something a little more like this:

1. Be aware and consider your thoughts
2. Take action by writing your thoughts on paper (or other methods of documentation) as they occur
3. Continue to focus and expand on the thoughts you have committed to paper
4. Take additional action by researching and continuing to actively write out your research and thoughts as they come to you
5. Take action by completing tasks that will help to develop the information you need to create and achieve your personal goals
6. When you have enough information, you can start filling in the elements to satisfy your SMART goals – or don't. Either way,

make sure you are completing tasks to work towards your goal

7. Create an action plan with a proposed (and flexible) timeline
8. Consider and write your thoughts and incoming information and continue to take action until your goal is achieved

The way to achieve results is by action. Without action, you will have no result and your ideas will not develop into goals. You cannot expect a specific goal to form without taking action to develop the information you need to create a goal. Napoleon Hill wrote in the book Think and Grow Rich that you do not need a plan to take action. When you take action, the plan comes together. Taking action is the necessary element of identifying, developing, and achieving a goal. Do not let the absence of a plan hold you back!

If you are consistently working towards your goal and lose sight of the SMART principle, good for you! You have officially identified the motivation you need to move forward. If you find yourself at a stand-still you may find that filling in the blanks that SMART goals provide will be what you need to motivate you to move forward. Again, do what works for you. It is not what works for someone else or because it is a generally accepted principle.

Unmet Versus Progression Goals

Just like most people who work for a large company or corporation, the goals I set at work need to meet the SMART criteria. However, many times, for reasons outside of our control, these goals are not met. A conversation with our managers helps to readjust these goals, but not without some extent of a connotation of failure. Although managers and employees are aware that these situations are sometimes unavoidable, not knowing details that tasks or actions reveal make initial time assessments nearly impossible to calculate with any accuracy.

I am not a psychologist. I do have an opinion that there is an unintended intrinsic feeling of failure when goals need to be changed or updated due to extenuating circumstances. Information that is received helps to clarify the metrics of a goal. However, when you initially set a goal you never have the breadth of information that you gain through the journey. Metrics in goal setting are supported with little more than a timeline (and budget, and resources...) that is ideal, but this estimate is based on the little knowledge that we are armed with at the beginning of a goal journey. The idea of changing goals implicating failure may also be a factor in lack of goal setting and, even more so, goal achieving. I don't know the answer to combat this connotation of failure in corporate goal setting. Getting a team, no matter how large, on the same page is a necessity. This common understanding is achieved by setting metrics for team goals. In our personal lives we have the flexibility to keep timelines and other metrics vague while we figure out the details. And when we do have more information to fill in the details, we *progress* in our goal journey. If we can populate this information, we now feel like we are getting tasks done as opposed to feeling like we have failed to meet an elusive and unknowingly unattainable estimate of a metric. We don't need to implement rigid timelines that may imply failure if not met, but can view updated information as progression and use it to fuel our motivation to achieve results.

The plan is fairly simple, and not at all rigid. The process allows for you to bend and flex the "rules" to allow your ideas to grow. Read on to understand the details of the suggested process and know that this plan is meant to be adjusted to be most efficient in YOUR life. Like I said, dirty it up to make a plan that works for you. Hopefully this strategy will help to make goal setting fun and easy for those of us who don't have an idea of what we already want to achieve and don't have the information to apply metrics.

CHAPTER 7

Brainstorm – Data Mine Your Thoughts

So, what are my goals?

Brainstorming is a tool typically used in a group setting for the purpose of solving an issue or creating a solution. Individual brainstorming involves taking this same process and making visual notes or drawings to cultivate ideas. From personal to work, individual or team, and corporate functions, brainstorming can be used in tasks such as determining your personal goals or a solution to a personal problem, identifying areas of improvement on your work team, and considering options for corporate initiatives, among many other uses.

Brainstorming can be fun and revealing, but it can also be demotivating and confusing when you don't have clarity about what you are looking to achieve. If you go into brainstorming with a world of possibilities (such as brainstorming possibilities for your undetermined personal goals) then brainstorming likely needs a little guidance and direction. There is a world of ideas to be considered and achieved. Narrowing down the possibilities when you have a few seeds of ideas is much easier to work with than it is to create a list from thin air. There has got to be (and there is) a way to identify a list of ideas that are relevant to our individual lives.

Unfortunately, goals don't reveal themselves to you just because you sat down at a desk with a pen and paper. Generally, a brainstorming session is a time you set aside to sit down and try to call forward thoughts. You cannot just call up amazing thoughts and ideas because you are ready to receive them. If this is an artform of yours, then you can skip this step and ultimately this book altogether.

In search of alternatives to brainstorming, or guidance to make my brainstorming sessions more fruitful, I turned to the internet. Much of the guidance that exists on the internet for finding your goals through brainstorming is a series of questions. The trigger questions I found were a variation of the following:

> *What am I passionate about?*
>
> *What do I spend my time talking about/researching?*
>
> *Where am I spending my money (helps identify your interests)?*
>
> *What book topics do you read?*
>
> *Who do I want to help?*
>
> *What problem do I want to solve?*
>
> *What were your childhood dreams?*
>
> *What topic lights up your face and your mood?*
>
> *What would you do with your time if money was no issue?*
>
> *What makes you feel fulfilled?*

If you are anything like me, your answers might look something like this:

> *What am I passionate about?* "Um, I don't know – isn't that what we are trying to figure out?"
>
> *What do I spend my time talking about/researching?* "Anything that will add value to my life" or the unfortunate common scenario

"anything that captures my attention on social media".

Where am I spending my money? "Monthly bills and retirement"

What book topics do you read? "Personal development, of course!"

Who do I want to help? "Myself...everybody?"

What problem do I want to solve? "I have no stinking clue – isn't that what we are trying to figure out here?"

What were your childhood dreams? "To have play dates with friends"

What topic lights up your face and your mood? "Vacation"

What would you do with your time if money was no issue? "Hmmmmm – probably be bored because everyone I spend my time with would still need to work. So I'll definitely keep my job."

What makes you feel fulfilled? "Again, isn't that what we are trying to figure out here?"

You get my drift. Although this guidance comes from a good place and can be useful in certain situations, these are questions that would require a lot of time, consideration, and soul searching (as well as tools and techniques to assist in consideration) in order for most of us to answer. Chances are that we would just give up and move on with living our autopilot life. I am not saying that these questions have no value. You can still keep these thought provoking questions in mind, but rather shift our focus to a technique that will help you to find these answers. Without additional guidance, useful and valuable answers to these questions are hard to come by.

If you go blank when posed these questions or get writer's block when you sit down at a desk to brainstorm and write goals, welcome to the club. So where could these ideas possibly be cultivated? The answer is easier than you think. The answers are hidden in a mess of thoughts that we overlook throughout the day – day after day after day. My suggestion is to data mine your own thoughts by becoming aware of and acknowledging these valuable nuggets of mental gold.

I am going to make a promise right here, right now. If you truly embrace the process in the following chapters, you will have a plethora of ideas you can build on – and if you listen to the signs from the universe, it will lead you on the right path to choose which goal(s) works for you at this point in your life. You have so many more thoughts and ideas in your brain than you realize, you just need to recognize the value of your thoughts and contemplate the possibilities they hold.

According to a 2020 study published by Julie Tseng and Jordan Poppenk, the average person has 6,200 thoughts a day. There is information regarding 70,000 thoughts a day, which many refer to, but I have not found any concrete studies that support the enormous figure (this does not mean that this number is incorrect, I just haven't found the supporting documentation). Many of these are likely random thoughts as the study did not focus on what people were thinking, but rather the *change* in thought. Using an MRI (magnetic resonance imaging) study, signals indicating changes in thought were identified and counted.

If our brains are this active, there is surely value and opportunity buried in those thoughts. I am willing to take a bet on you that at least one of these thoughts might give you the start to an amazing journey. The reason these thoughts have not been of much value to us in the past is that we allow these thoughts to come to us, we acknowledge that we will consider or think about it later and move on. These thoughts tend to come back to us time and again. Instead of acting on the ideas, we just stay in this cycle of thinking and dismissing ideas that have the potential of becoming amazing goals, and eventually achievements. Let's change that cycle.

Brainstorming Process

The brainstorming process consists of three basic steps; thought capture, consideration, and critique. In this chapter we will discuss the first step in capture. Capturing your ideas or thoughts is a two-step process that warrants discussion. During thought or idea capture you really want to consider all thoughts that come to you that could be formed into goals. Capturing thoughts should follow a basic lack of rules in that brainstorming should be an all-inclusive no judging zone, should encourage wild and crazy ideas, encourage building onto basic ideas, and encourage quantity over quality. The overall process looks like the drawing below, but we will be focusing on the first step in capture in this chapter.

Data mining your thoughts is a simple process, with the most challenging aspect being that you must allow thoughts to come to you and be flexible and aware when they present. Once you capture these thoughts, the next steps of considering and critiquing are where you get to be creative and consider all your possibilities.

When and Where to Brainstorm?

We all have times when we find our minds wandering with random thoughts. One of my favorite times to brainstorm is when I am exercising. Actively using my body, but not so much my brain. This is not something that I alone use, as many people choose to exercise when their minds are on overdrive and they need to work through their thoughts. Other great times to be aware of our thoughts for the purpose of brainstorming are during menial tasks such as stuffing envelopes, folding papers, or vacuuming the house. I will add driving in the car to the list of great data mining moments, with the caveat that you have got to be creative about how you document these thoughts – safety first!

Don't be fooled and therefore unprepared as the times you plan to brainstorm are not the only times that great thoughts will present themselves. If you are unprepared, your valuable thoughts may slip your mind before you can bring them to the next step of capture. You can be in the middle of a work meeting (completely inconvenient) and a comment made or an image seen will trigger a thought. Now is not the time to consider this thought further, but a quick note will help you to remember your thoughts later in the day when it is convenient. I am easily triggered to develop thoughts while I am reading or listening to audio books, related or unrelated to the content. It's a time when my brain is building my perception of the words and the theories presented. This is also the time when my thoughts are most evasive, so I am very disciplined at pausing and documenting my thoughts immediately. Brainstorming during these other activities is a purposeful and effective use of multitasking. Learning to employ effective multitasking can be an amazing skill. Multitasking (much like the word "dirty") is not always a good thing. In fact, in many situations multitasking leaves you unfocused and less effective. Multitasking is attempting to perform two tasks concurrently, which means that neither task has your undivided attention. However, when one task you are performing does not require much brain power (like exercise), multitasking to data mine your thoughts during this same time is a useful and effective use of your time. Think about it – if people have a lot on their minds, many use exercise or taking a drive to clear their heads. Learn to listen and be aware of the thoughts in your head. The best part about this form of multitasking is that you tend to get lost in your thoughts and the finish line of your workout or task appears without much notice. Time flies when you get lost in your thoughts – or rather find yourself in your thoughts. You will come to see these thoughts, turned into words on paper, are the magic seeds that great goals and accomplishments are made. Stop being one of the many people who experience these thoughts and dismiss them just as quickly. With a single breath out you can release a great thought. This is the death of a great idea – the one that could have gotten you to your next level of potential and fulfillment.

Meditation

Not meditation! I'm with you, I have never been a fan. I owe the day I changed my perception to Kristen Brown and Instagram. Kristen is from my small hometown. She is an entrepreneur, a motivational speaker, yoga therapist, author, and mother – and those are only the accomplishments I know about.

She posed a question to ask her followers what topics they would like to hear more about on her podcast. Being into this type of energy work, I decided to respond, which is very out of character for me. I responded with a list of practices I enjoyed but made sure to mention that I dislike meditation. It's what I added in after that comment that had me contemplating meditation for days after I responded. I wrote to her "but it feels good at the end of my yoga workout to enjoy the relaxation of savasanah or corpse pose". I do. I just lay there feeling my body and letting my mind be blank for a minute – and by a minute, I probably mean 45 seconds. This was the day I changed my perspective in regard to meditation.

It was this interaction that prompted the realization that meditation is not what I perceived it to be. Turns out that you can dirty up meditation to fit your liking too! My original understanding of meditation was sitting on the ground, crossing legs, boarding straight posture, staring into my eyelids for hours on end, and constantly shooing thoughts out of my mind. Oh, and I'm supposed to dismiss that itch?! Almost anywhere you look, the definition of meditation is a set of techniques to heighten awareness and focus the mind. Nowhere in the definition does it indicate the length of time, body position, or location to experience meditation.

Meditation can be an excellent time to brainstorm. When you are completely relaxed and allow your brain to let go of stress and worries and just be present in the moment, you are also allowing your brain to wander freely. Worry and stress limit creativity and opportunity. Focusing your thoughts on your stress and worry does not provide solutions and does not provide comfort. But allowing your thoughts to be free and help you create opportunities, that is where your solutions and ideas for your goals are generated. Make meditation a fun, worry-free, stress-free zone for you to enjoy. The potential you create for brainstorming during your mental vacation of meditation may just be some of the best ideas you identify.

CONSIDER THIS:

Meditation allows thoughts to flow without expectation. Forcing thoughts = Writer's block. Scheduling time to brainstorm may put you in a situation where you feel you need to force your thoughts. Meditation is complete relaxation with no expectations, but the potential for great opportunities.

What thoughts are worth acknowledging?

We have so many passive thoughts that run through our heads every day. Some have little or no value to us or anyone else, but some have major potential of turning into a fun and fulfilling personal goal. For the purposes of data mining our thoughts to develop goals, we generally have three types of thoughts to decipher:

1. Chatter/Static – our minds work at speeds we cannot comprehend. These types of thoughts are a general way for us to work our way through life scenarios. Chatter can be helpful or hurtful, depending on how we train ourselves to deal with situations. They can be a running script of worry, overthinking, consideration, contemplation, and reflection on a more positive note. Chatter is generally an inner dialogue to process one's circumstances.
2. Observation – this is a detail that has captured our attention. We identify with the thought we are processing and move on or contemplate what we have observed.

3. Vision/Possible Goals - These are thoughts and ideas that can be turned into goals. They can be random thoughts that you capture as they pop into your head, or they can be a thought that has progressed as a result of an observation.

Chatter is rarely something that will turn into a vision, or goal, thought. So much chatter really can't even be collected into full thought, but that doesn't mean it can't happen. Here are a few thoughts of my own (or seeded by conversations with my boyfriend) that have made it through to thoughts that could be documented and considered:

Thought progression example 1

Chatter: "I need to rent a cart for golfing. My shoulder hurts when walking my bag."

Observation: "A golf bike? What an interesting concept."

Vision: "If a golf bike works, I wonder if a scooter would be an option"

Captured thought: "Golf scooter" (FYI, these already exist – but you wouldn't know if you didn't do the research)

Thought progression example 2

> Chatter: "This duvet cover is such a pain to take off
> and put on. I hate having to wash it."
>
> Observation: "There has got to be an easier way."
>
> Vision: "What if there was a duvet cover that was
> more of a pocket than a bag"
>
> Captured thought: "Duvet pocket" (FYI, I have not
> found that this exists, but am working on it!)

Thought progression example 3

> **Chatter:** "Free return. If I don't like it I will just ship
> it \back."
>
> **Observation:** "Companies must spend a fortune on
> returns"
>
> **Vision:** "I wonder if reverse or honest advertising
> would limit returns?" (In my research, I found that
> brick and mortar stores have an 8% return rate,
> while internet shopping is around the 33% range.
> Shipping return costs are a large expense for
> internet-based companies).
>
> **Captured thought:** "Reverse or review based
> advertising to limit returns, including the admitting
> to the downside where this product may not be the
> best option" (FYI...I have looked into this in a
> limited way and sent an email to a company that

might benefit from the idea as it's not something that is in my wheelhouse, or really interesting to me).

Obviously, a thought such as "I really like her shirt" isn't something that you would capture. But if your thought progresses to "that is a great shirt, but it would be really great in a different fit" or "I should modify that shirt to fit my taste" - is an example of a thought that could be formed into a goal. If your idea provides something for you to consider the solutions to a problem, a different perspective on an old solution, or options of achieving something new, then you may have found the basis for a personal goal.

Realistic

Do you know that you are limitless? Beliefs that only realistic things are possible are what hold us back from greatness. We all have a tendency to be naysayers when we don't believe in the possibilities in life. We ease the burden on ourselves by agreeing that something is impossible and moving on. We deny ourselves the gift of innovation and exploration. Automatically deferring to impossibilities limits our imagination and ultimately limits our lives.

Doesn't the option of believing you are limitless sound so much more exciting than being a prisoner of the limits of your beliefs that hold you back? Your thoughts are the raw data. Raw data that, through the process outlined in this book, will evolve into something that is possible. Your initial idea might sound impossible, but with a little consideration and research, these ideas have the ability to become a reality.

A simple idea has the potential of becoming a massive achievement. And a ridiculous idea, well that too has the potential to evolve into something great. Do you know that several inventions we use today were found by mistake while working on a different goal or invention? Products as simple as saccharine, silly putty, and potato chips to products as complex as microwaves, fireworks, and pacemaker implants for the heart were all discovered while working toward another idea or goal. I don't really agree with the statement that these products were mistakes because they were achievements that evolved out of working toward a goal. These are products that are used every day and are massive success stories. These products evolved out of thought and action. Now is your opportunity to move that simple or ridiculous idea to the next stage and watch it evolve.

There are two important key takeaways in this chapter; capture as much as possible and avoid dismissing ideas before giving them time and consideration to evolve. We will now focus on the second phase of capturing these thoughts by taking notes and allowing ideas to blossom. Don't be hindered by your notion of reality. Don't we already know that reality bites? And missing out on an opportunity or possibility due to reality – that really bites! So capture those thoughts and let's get to the action.

CHAPTER 8

Take Action

Take Action – Write your goals

We are programmed over repeated interactions in which we are exposed in high school, college, and throughout our careers and lives to believe that goals need to be a set of specific and complete details to take action. We are trained that goals are not sufficient until they are put in some variation of a SMART format. In reality, goals start with an initial idea, followed by substantial thought and consideration, research, discussion, and planning before they ever evolve into a formatted, specific goal. There are some elements that take time to reveal themselves and occur as a result of action taken before the idea is complete enough to set a SMART goal. Opposed to traditional thinking, a lack of specific details or timeframes does not mean you don't have a goal, and it doesn't mean that you can't start taking action to work toward answers and an end-result.

This is the point in the process of the widely accepted sequence of goal setting, where conventional thinking tells you to set SMART GOALS. I might be an underachiever in this regard, but when journeying through goal discovery I wouldn't have most of the details to provide a valuable answer to the questions I need to make a goal SMART. But I don't agree with the argument that my goal is not yet a goal, AND I am absolutely not going to wait to take action until my goals are SMART. Call me crazy, but I believe taking action on your goals before you have all the details will only help to identify the elements of SMART goals that are missing. I am okay with having a goal that does not meet the criteria that the goal experts suggest my goals need to meet. I also believe that setting specific metrics without gathering information that taking action provides is dangerous to the mental aspect of achieving goals. When you fail to meet your goals because your details were based on uneducated and uninformed lack of information, you introduce an increased possibility of failure, which may deter people from continuing their journey.

Say you have a goal of making a flying car like we remember from the Jetson's. Much like Elon Musk's goal of achieving life on Mars, the concept of a flying car may include goals of several individual milestones to finally get to the flying car, and the details will most definitely change along the journey. But if you don't start taking steps to get there and achieving these milestones, the details you need to get to the flying car will not be uncovered. The process of working towards milestones is to identify the details you need to achieve your goals. Eventually, I do imagine that our cars are going to continue to evolve into something different than they are right now. I am all for not having to buy another set of tires!

This second step in capturing ideas and thoughts as part of brainstorming is really the action of capturing your thoughts to form ideas and goals. Recognizing and data mining our thoughts (brainstorming) is only the first step in capturing our thoughts. The key to an effective brainstorming element is immediate action through documentation or physically writing your goals on paper. The sequence looks like this:

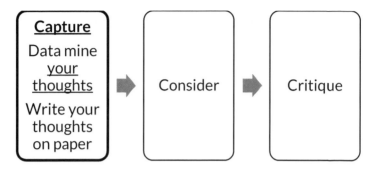

Mental notes do not work. Mental notes are elusive and limiting. When an idea is presenting itself to you, that idea may keep popping into your head in an altered form, or it may flea never to be captured in the same or very similar context to which it had presented itself initially. Rolf Smith said it best when he stated "the problem with mental notes is that the ink fades very rapidly". When a thought presents itself, write it down on paper. What happens is truly amazing. It's like your mind is relieved of trying to hold onto the thought and even advances the thought by expanding into additional thoughts that form a solid idea. The mushrooming effect of writing a single thought, and then continuing to capture subsequent thoughts, is exciting and motivating. Continuing to write these thoughts on paper releases the grip that your mind has on a single thought and allows the idea to blossom into a goal.

There are a few out there that have incredible memories and can recall information stored for a period of time, but most of us have trouble remembering specific details, much less recalling what we thought about throughout the day. As much as you think you have things organized in your brain, when you write your thoughts out in ink the missing details become visible. Imagine applying for a loan to start a business with the Small Business Association and expecting them to approve your loan with no business plan or supporting documentation to demonstrate your ability to pay off the loan.

Do you think mental notes and a verbal account of plans would be acceptable? Or imagine your general contractor showing up to build your dream home and he tells you that he has no drawn plans for the house he is building for you but he has a clear picture in his head of what he is going to build. I imagine you would be panicking. Do you think the SBA would lend you money for your business or would you be willing to take a chance on your general contractor to build your dream home to your expectations? Both scenarios are set-ups for failure and can be easily mitigated by creating written plans that clearly define the research, findings, and next steps that go into these projects.

Now apply the frivolous act of relying on your brain and memory to document your thoughts and develop personal goals. You are more likely to get farther and be successful with your personal goals if you write them on paper. The simple process of writing is action. The first action. Once you take that action, other actions will follow and snowball into momentum, which will take hold and continue throughout your goal journey. I don't want you to wait until you have solid details that you can document before you start writing or taking any other action. Your goals are going to come from your thoughts and the actions you take on those thoughts. Your thoughts and actions are going to blossom into details that will fuel your goals.

Always Be Composing/Writing

Alec Baldwin has a notable scene in the 1992 film *Glengarry Glen Ross* where he is presenting an ultimatum to a real estate team to either improve their performance or get fired. Using the acronym ABC – Always Be Closing, he drove home the expectation that each individual needs to be focused on closing deals every day. I'm not sure how successful his less than motivational (more so threatening) speech was, but the message behind the speech works well for our purposes. Feel free to go onto YouTube and check out the scene – it's also fun to see so many amazing actors earlier in their careers. When this principle is applied to our actions for developing our thoughts into goals, I suggest a different meaning for the acronym ABC.

A – Always

B – Be

C – Composing (writing)

The act of writing can never hurt you (unless you are documenting a crime or other indiscretion you committed, which could end you in hot water or jail), but it can help you in multiple ways. If we take measures to make sure we are always prepared to take action by writing, those actions will turn into results.

I know that this step seems like a no-brainer. It is a no-brainer. However, I bet this scenario is familiar - you get to the grocery store, no list in hand (or you decided you would remember that one single item you didn't have time to write down) and you go home without the mental item and a new grocery list that started before you even finished the full task of a grocery run.

The same thing is guaranteed to happen with your goals. You really don't quite believe in the extensive value the simple task of writing holds, so you let the task or action slip. And those thoughts – that had such potential to grow – are gone. There were a few times during the writing of this book where I was sure I would remember because writing was not convenient. I know that the loss of those ideas would have changed and enhanced parts of this book. There will be times when you will miss important thoughts – just don't make it a habit. Have a plan to capture thoughts during inconvenient times.

Motivation Process

Getting started always seems to be the hardest part. But once you take the first step, the following steps seem to come much more easily. In the same film, Glengarry Glen Ross, Alec's character also used the acronym AIDA -Attention, Interest, Decision, and Action – to detail the motivation sequence that will get the team to ABC. Applying the AIDA principles from the video to identify and develop your goals:

A - *I have your attention because you have already realized that you want to set personal goals. I know this because you picked up this book.*

I - You are interested because you have made it this far into the book.

D - *Make and commit to the decision to move forward with identifying and developing your personal goals.*

A - *Now put that decision into action by getting out your pen and paper or making your phone/computer accessible at all times. By doing so, you can start to document your thoughts and develop your goals and Always Be Composing.*

Just find the motivation to start. Once you start, the following steps will fall into place as you get excited by the outcome and motivated to continue on your personal goal journey. Once the thoughts start rolling, the action of writing not only helps you to remember, it also helps to organize and reveal missing information. Another effect is that it releases your hold on the original thought to allow you to focus on new emerging thoughts. This theory is known as the Zeigarnik Effect. The Zeigarnik Effect is the theory that we keep pulling undone tasks into our awareness. When we write these bits of information down, it has a similar effect as completing the task. Because we know these tasks are accounted for on paper, we release the burden on our memory and allow our thoughts to focus on the current task.

The Invaluable Aha Moment

If we are always composing/writing, we will become more aware of our opportunities and create aha moments. Aha moments are epiphanies that are the collision of perception, new information, and a moment where your mind is open to new ideas. Aha moments change our perceptions and can only create results if you are motivated to take action when the event is realized. The value of aha moments are reciprocal:

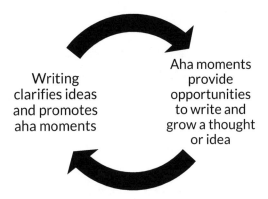

Having a plan to write, review and expand on these thoughts provides opportunities to learn and grow throughout the entire goal process. Thoughts accompanied by the action of writing are the building blocks to making a series of aha moments that intentionally evolve into achievable goals.

An additional benefit of the aha moments is that when you change your perception of an element, your brain is willing to consider how this affects other aspects of the ideas you had been holding as true. You open up space in your mind to consider and recognize how your goals have been affected and new ideas start emerging. This is the essence of the evolution of goals. New information influences direction and outcomes. The effect of new direction and outcomes will be discussed when we consider and critique our ideas in the next chapters. Ultimately, we adjust as we need to and keep our goals on track. It might be a new track, or a different track than expected, but on track, nonetheless.

The Proof is in the Writing

My experience with this process overall has been that the act of writing makes me more aware and gets me thinking strategically. Not just about one specific topic (insert goal), it changes my thinking patterns about other topics and opens up my mind to ideas and information on many different subjects. Effective practice of the Take Action concept is to keep a pen and paper or your phone handy and write down or document thoughts as they occur. For ultimate success with this plan, you need to be prepared for the second step of writing your thoughts at any moment. The evolution of your thoughts is the catalyst for continued motivation and evolution of your goal. And the evolution of your thoughts is dependent on capturing your new and advanced thoughts as they occur.

If you are not yet convinced of the power of a simple action of writing your thoughts, give it a try.

There are several ways to implement the action of writing in your daily activities that will impact your life in different ways. The following are life hack suggestions that have been used by psychologists, life coaches, and staple advice from those in our lives we turn to for guidance:

Write out your "To Do" list

Make a complete list of things you need to get done around the house (inclusive of your chores, errands, and any other miscellaneous tasks like transporting kiddos) and/or at your job for the day. The act of writing this list on paper will ensure that you don't forget to do the task later, and also free up your mind so you can focus on getting one task done at a time. Aside from these benefits, there is a welcome feeling of satisfaction with every task you get to cross off your list as you complete them. If you write your to-do list, you will get more done throughout the day making you more efficient. In a Forbes article from 2019, a To Do list was number 10 in the article with the author commenting that the use of this list was his favorite life hack for work.

Take Action / / /

Write your feelings and emotions to get stress off your mind

If you have something that has been on your mind and stealing your peace and happiness, try writing it down and see if you feel more at ease. If you write out feelings or thoughts that have been bothering you on paper, you will be more likely to let go of whatever feeling it is that you have been holding onto. This includes writing a letter to someone that you have been wanting or needing to clear the air. Instead of sending it, shred it. Many times we don't even need to talk to the person we have an issue with, we just need to vent and let the steam out. Get your feelings on paper so you can let them go. These negative feelings only hurt yourself, not anyone else. Do whatever you can to rid yourself of this negativity.

This is something I practiced when I was dealing with negative thoughts from being on Facebook (why is it that we all feel crummy after using this platform, but we all keep using it?). The things good people are willing to say when behind a keyboard and screen are truly shocking. And then other good people argue back when participating in these social media conversations is futile. I know I am not the only person affected by this behavior. Instead of replying, I go over my reply time and time again in my head – which really is no better than replying in anger on the platform because it affects my mood until I can let it go. Before I made a great decision to substantially minimize my use of Facebook (we've all got to creep sometimes, right?), I got in the habit of writing my response out on my computer and then deleting it. Guess what?! I was able to let go of the negative script in my head and move on with my day. It truly is an amazing tool if you take the time to practice it.

Keep a notepad by your bed

Another popular suggestion for people who cannot sleep due to their running minds, or who are trying to create, is to keep a notepad by your bed. Getting these thoughts out of your head and onto paper helps in both releasing thoughts so you can fall asleep, and for documenting ideas or thoughts that you may want to consider and expand on in the morning or in the future. The notes app on your phone is an option, but remember it is never a good suggestion to keep your phone in your bedroom, or at least not right next to your bed. Additionally, picking up your phone while you are trying to sleep can draw you into a series of events that have you checking your notifications, which prompts you to take other actions on your phone and keeps you further from your goal of sleep.

Daily Journaling

Journaling is something that I did not implement in my life until this year. I had tried to keep a diary as a teenager, but didn't find much benefit in it and wondered why I would ever want to go back and reminisce over what I did every day. I did not understand what to write in a journal, nor did I understand the value of the concept overall. In my current journaling practice, I write my thoughts, tasks I want to complete for the day to work toward my goals, my affirmations, and five things for which I am grateful. The grateful list helps me to recognize that even the challenges in life are beneficial, and the little things in life add up to make life great. The benefits of daily journaling help organize thoughts, track ideas, and get thoughts and feelings on paper so you can free up time and space in your mind.

Any one of these are a good option for recognizing the value of writing out our thoughts and feelings in our daily lives. Give just one, or any combination of them, a try and see what benefits you can identify in your own life.

Fit the Plan to Fit Your Life

Capturing your ideas is a flexible practice that you can adjust to fit your style. If you are on the road driving for your job, or other personal reasons, writing your thoughts on paper is a dangerous option. However, most of us have a smartphone and some sort of connectivity in our cars that enable us to send text messages. Create a contact for yourself on your phone so you can easily voice command your car/phone to send yourself a text message of your thoughts. If you have a pretty good memory and all you need is one or two words to remind you of your thoughts, then keep it simple. If one or two words will draw a blank for you, then make sure you take more descriptive notes. I prefer the act of writing out my thoughts with pen and paper over any other method, but when I am walking my dogs, my phone is what I have available. Sometimes I am already on my computer, so I just type my notes there, as eventually my notes that I expand on typically end up on my computer anyway. If you are a weightlifter who tracks reps and weights, you already have a pen and paper handy so why not jot notes at the same time as you document your exercise? The method of documentation also changes with the goal for which I am taking notes.

My bedding ideas and physical resolutions get documented on paper initially and only transferred, if necessary, while any notes for my book get transferred to my computer within the day. Have a plan for documentation but be flexible so you have a method of documentation available at all times that fits with your daily schedule.

CONSIDER THIS:

Observation of your thoughts + writing your thoughts = Effective brainstorming for developing goals

Idea documentation Tool

I have included a template to document your thoughts below. You can download this template from my website AlynMitlyng.com. This is included to give you a general concept of how you might document and evolve your thoughts. The top line labeled *Idea:* is where you will want to write the main thought you are going to expand. The lines below the idea heading are for the ideas that mushroom from your initial thought. There are separate sections for multiple main ideas, as you may want to document multiple thoughts and see where your thought journey takes you.

The thought you originally thought you may want to work toward may not develop the way another thought does, so you may shift your focus as you travel the path to determining and setting your goals. There is a column on the right side to document actions that you can use as either a to do list, or as documentation to help develop thoughts in relation to those ideas.

At the end of each idea section is a line to write your goal as it comes together. Remember, this goal does not need to be specific, just something basic that documents any details that you have at the time. You are welcome to write your SMART acronym on paper to document those specifics as they become available or as they change. And remember – changes to goals should be seen as progress, not failure.

IDEA DEVELOPMENT TOOL

Idea:

NOTE:	ACTION:

GOAL:

Idea:

NOTE:	ACTION:

GOAL:

Again, the format in the Idea Development Tool is just one suggestion. You can bend and flex to fit your motivation and style. The most important task is getting your thoughts on paper or into written word of some format. Writing our thoughts on paper is such an important step, I thought it constituted another chapter. Shall we continue?

.

CHAPTER 9

Thought Action Process

Consider Your Captured Thoughts

Writing is a continual process throughout your goal journey. You don't stop the practice at writing down just the original thought, or when you have a substantial goal. To be really effective, you keep writing and building on these thoughts to carry you throughout the entire process. There is no guarantee your thoughts will still be lurking when you finally set aside time to write them on paper, and you need these progressive thoughts to help you get to an end result. Continuing through the brainstorming process, we are now at the point where we will consider the information we have captured:

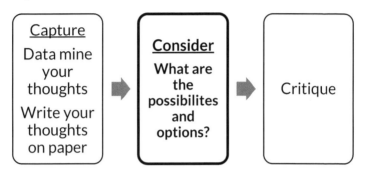

By now you have captured some thoughts without a filter of judgement and without dismissing wild and crazy thoughts. Without a filter, every crazy idea that went through your head...well, they all should have made it onto your Idea Documentation Tool, or other note taking method. In the brainstorming step of consideration, consider the possibilities of your original thoughts. Do not let the thoughts of impossibilities cloud your creativity and prevent you from pursuing amazing opportunities.

We want to focus on developing these initial thoughts and ideas into something that is a unique goal. So, we continue to write our mushrooming thoughts until our minds create an idea that is unique and achievable. I know I have said that you are limitless (you are) but achieving certain goals (like flying) takes time, ideas, and innovation to make it achievable. You are not going to help someone fly just by telling them to flap their arms really hard and fast. But there are opportunities for innovation that will help people fly, you just have to figure that out. That is the purpose of putting additional thought and action into considering the *how* of our ideas.

When considering your brainstorming ideas and notes, the purpose is to determine what opportunities can be identified in the thoughts you have captured. So often we automatically go toward the narrative that our ideas are silly, or too much work, or something we will put on the backburner for later. There are two main questions that you should be asking yourself in the consideration phase. The questions are:

1. What are the possibilities of this idea?
2. What are my options to make a version of this happen?

The answers will likely not come to you immediately when you pose these questions. But in those moments when you are brainstorming, focus your thoughts and attention to how you can answer these questions to make your idea possible, and what additional ideas can contribute to making the idea happen. Your brain is an amazing machine that will provide the answers to the possibilities and options. Remember that your continuing to write your thoughts will help to iron out the details.

A word of caution in this phase: we lean on the internet a lot for answers and direction on the validity of our goals. The many places you look will guide you through a series of questions like the following:

- Does the potential goal address a problem that needs to be fixed?
- Is my idea something that will improve life, a process, or make a task easier?
- Are there other solutions out there that can more easily and quickly get you to your goal?
- What are others' opinions about your goal?

The idea is that if your answer is yes to the first two questions, no to the third question, and mostly positive feedback to the last question, your idea or goal is worth additional consideration. But I argue that even if you answer these questions and they negate the value of your goal, your goal may still hold amazing potential that these questions dismiss. The question above that I dislike the most is considering others' opinions about your goal. Here is just one example of why: I reached out to my cousin one night to ask him about his experience as an innovator. My cousin is an amazing, supportive, always happy, and motivated human. He is always supportive and is always kind, so I do understand his intentions in our exchange. When I told him about my bedding idea, he excitedly asked me if I had tried the duvet cover from Costco, as they have a really nice one that works really well – maybe I don't need to make a new one?

He was just trying to offer a solution that he had found and had a good experience using. His response could have easily been taken as a dismissal of the value of my idea. I did not take his response that way, I know him too well to know that he was trying to be helpful. The issue I dislike with traditional duvet covers is not something that he has appreciated. That does not mean that there are not others out there who have the same frustrations I do. Every person has a different experience with different products.

You don't need to look very far to find confirmation of this fact. Find any product on the World Wide Web and read the reviews – there are very few products out there (I would argue next to none) that have the same realized benefit to everyone. A solution for one person may not be ideal for the next due to preferences or experience. Had I not understood this, I may have quickly scrapped my idea. Multiple solutions exist for a single problem, and not one solution works for every person. Take others' opinions in stride. Consider and keep moving forward.

I am in awe of people who believe in limitless possibilities. Those who create ideas and shoot for the moon time after time. I have no idea to the extent of what is possible in this world, and who am I to say if something is impossible or worth consideration. If someone shares an idea or vision with me, I always get excited about the possibilities with them. That is not everyone's view, so be careful to not listen to those prompting caution and extinguishing your excitement. Henry Ford is quoted as saying "If I had asked people what they wanted, they would have said faster horses." Many people need to ease into the idea of possibilities – and that is okay. But you and I, let's be among those that believe that limits are only in our minds and possibilities are yet to be discovered.

CONSIDER THIS:

If an idea or thought seems impossible, try looking at it from a different perspective. If you catch yourself thinking that you can't, or the idea is impossible, keep it in the cycle and carry it through the process of consideration and critiquing. You never know what possibilities might appear!

Moving forward through this process, remember that if you get stuck or run into challenges, there is a way to move forward with your goal. Considering the impossibilities will get you nowhere. Focus on the challenges you are facing and start back during the initial brainstorming process to capture your thoughts on your challenge. Document these focused thoughts to identify the possibilities that will help you through the challenge. The great thing about this time around is that you have a specific topic or challenge you are brainstorming, so you do not have the pressure of narrowing your search from a world of possibilities. The magic contained in a general idea carried through this goal development process will change your thought process from all the reasons an idea can't work to figuring out how it can work. Trust the process and forget the rest. What do you have to lose?

Through this process you will notice that brainstorming is a constant cycle. It is a myth that brainstorming is a technique that happens only at the beginning of a project, or to develop an initial thought. Brainstorming is a technique that you will use repeatedly throughout the process of developing, evolving, and achieving your goals. It is very redundant as you data mine your thoughts and take action by writing your thoughts. More thoughts, write your thoughts, research, write your discoveries and thoughts about your research, more thought, document your thoughts by writing. Thoughts and research do not remain in your memory. Continue to be aware of and write out your thoughts no matter where you are in the process.

Critique and Adjust As Needed

The final step in brainstorming is to critique. When you critique your brainstorming results you will modify and adjust the aspects of your thoughts that will help you in moving forward with your goal. For those areas that are still presenting a challenge, you will repeat the process until a solution for that challenge has been identified – from capturing, to considering, to critiquing your focused thoughts. All of these steps are beautifully orchestrated in your brain as the first time through, they will happen in order and on time. As you progress through your goals, you may find yourself capturing one aspect while you are critiquing and adjusting another idea and reconsidering the possibilities of the results of your critique. The neatly organized brainstorming process looks something like this:

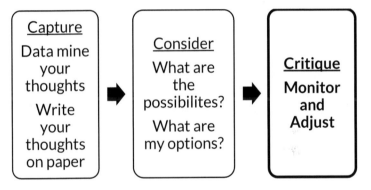

Thought Action Process

This continual and cyclically accepted process of brainstorming that helps you to develop your ideas into goals is something I refer to as the Thought Action Process or "TAP(ping) into your goals". The brainstorming process of capture, consider, critique is a method in our world of psychology that is used to describe the brainstorming process. The Thought Action Process is the orchestrated use of this method that harmonizes the steps in the brainstorming process. When developing your goals using the Dirty Method, you will TAP into your goals using the following progression:

Thought
- Data mine your thoughts

Action
- Write your thoughts on paper or equivalent

Process
- Advance or Archive thoughts and ideas

Thought
- Use your continued thoughts to build on a single idea

Action
- Continue to write, research, and take identified actions

Process
- Advance your goal and Archive that which isn't relevant now

Thought
- Use collection of thoughts to develop goal

Action
- Continue to document and take action to progress in your goal

Process
- Develop fluid action plan to achieve your goal

Flexible (Dirty) rules for TAP (ping) into your goals:

1. Any thought that presents a possibility – write it down.
2. Don't dismiss an idea because it sounds silly in your head. When you write it on paper you have taken action with that thought. Your mind will do the work to make that silly idea transform into something realistic and possible.
3. In the moments, days and weeks following these thoughts, write down follow-up thoughts you have about the idea to help your idea develop and grow.
4. Take additional action on the thoughts you write down. Through research and discovery your goal will form. As you continue to take action, you will work toward developing and achieving your goals at the same time.
5. Don't waste time on any of your thoughts that don't light a spark inside of you. If you can think about it, it is possible in some form. Your subconscious revealed the thought to you for a reason. Write it down and see if your mind and thoughts do the work to expand on the idea to make it something that excites you.

6. If the SMART (or similar) method is motivating to you, document specific details when you have enough information. Remember, you don't need detail to take action, so don't wait for these details to reveal themselves first.

7. When a specific detail of a goal changes, regard it as progress and keep moving. Having to change the details of a goal may have a connotation of failure – that is not the case with your personal dirty goals. Information is in progress. If you have to change the details a third, fourth or fifth time, that is still just more progress.

8. Make the action plan fluid. When a goal changes due to information collected, you want the action plan to be flexible to fit those changes (this will be discussed further in the next chapter).

The term TAP into your goals suggests that these goals are already in you. Your potential, unlimited success, fulfillment, happiness – it is all stored in your brain. The culmination of your experience and passion for purposes not yet discovered are all up there waiting for you to implement the tools to let out those passions. You don't have to rummage through a world of ideas to create a goal, as there are so many possibilities that can be captured in the form of your thoughts. Once you turn on the TAP, the ideas and thoughts to develop your goals will flow to you like water from a faucet. As long as you keep acknowledging and transferring your thoughts onto paper, the faucet will keep flowing. For the cost of paper and a pen you can take a journey through your brain and TAP into your thoughts to discover your goals.

Goal Documentation Tool

Much like the Idea Documentation Tool presented in Chapter 8, the following Goal Documentation Tool is for documenting your mushrooming thoughts and ideas about your goal as it progresses. It is the same document, only modified for the advancement of the process. When you have a goal in mind, the details of that goal will evolve. This document will help you rewrite your goals often to make sure you are on course, and to capture any changes in the details of your goals as you gain information.

The top line labeled *Goal:* is where you will want to write the basic goal you are working toward. You can use this template in two ways, however, the intention of the design is to be able to easily evaluate the progression of your goal through the second option:

- Use the separate sections for different goals if you are working on more than one goal at a time
- Use the separate sections to rewrite the same personal goals on the top line as goals progress and details are obtained

The lines below the Goal heading are for the progress in action and thoughts that help drive you to your details and achievement of personal goals. You can use this document as a version of a scratch pad which you can then transfer to whatever method you are using to document the journey of each of your goals. Or you can use it as a central documentation location. On the last section of this worksheet, I have added the letters for the acronym SMART as a place where you can detail changes in the metrics of your goals. When considering the details of achievable, don't think of that detail as a yes or no, but rather a search for the answer of how it will be achievable. The action column remains on this form as well, once again for the purposes of a to do list, or as documentation to help indicate work completed in relation to your personal goals. Always remember that changes to goals should be seen as progress, not failure.

Goal Development Tool

Goal:

NOTE/TASK: **ACTION:**

Goal:

NOTE/TASK: **ACTION:**

S(pecific):
M(easurable):
A(chievable):
R(ealistic):
T(ime based):

The previous is only one suggestion for those who prefer some sort of template. I prefer to keep written notes in a notebook with a method that keeps the flow going forward to avoid the need to flip back on the pages to make additional notes where the original thought occurred. Once I act on something I like to put a single line through it (some like a checkmark next to it) so I can always refer back and reconsider previous thoughts. My notebook looks something like this:

Thoughts

Linen cover idea I have had for years — explore opportunity

Information is very limited on determining goals

Write a book on developing goals — figure out a method

So many options, how do I limit

~~Add notebook to grocery list~~

How do SMART goals apply

SMART goals — how? I have no details

SMART goals — wait to take action until you have a plan — too excited to wait.

SMART goals — necessary for business, not necessarily for personal?

So limiting!!

<u>Goal: Write a book on determining your goals</u>

~~Chapter Ideas:~~

~~Miracle Morning Journey~~

~~Intro~~

~~Accepted goal process.~~

~~Chapters on alternative methods such as:~~

~~Brainstorming alternatives~~

~~Taking action before a goal is even a goal, much less SMART~~

~~Benefits of having goals~~

~~What prevents us from setting achieving goals?~~

Write whatever thoughts come to your mind, with however much information you need to make your notes clear and understandable to you. Eventually, all of these items on my list were crossed off, but not until I incorporated them into my outline and written text. I know that my notes above don't mean anything to you, but I clearly understand what I was trying to capture. Review your notes from day to day to make sure that you make use of or discard the information accordingly. Use these notes to create an action plan which we will discuss in the next chapter. If you are anything like me and like to dirty up your life to fit your motivation, you may have already gotten to a version of this next step. Don't worry, an action plan does not have to be a big formal document, but it will be as extensive as you need to carry you through the process of developing and achieving your goals.

CHAPTER 10

Create an Action Plan

Progressive Thought Action Process

Data mining your thoughts and writing them down to develop ideas through brainstorming is the first part of this process. But remember, our mission is to develop and achieve personal goals as a result of the entire process. In the previous chapters you took action by writing your ideas on paper. You continue to take action by doing research to help develop your ideas and make an ink or pencil note of that information as well. At this point, you likely have enough information to start filling in some of the blanks required for a SMART goal.

As a reminder, these are not rigid rules, but rather guides to keep you on task and in line with the desired end result. With the power of knowledge and information that you gain from taking action, your thoughts will evolve into goals as you work through the goal achievement process. Dirty goals are less rigid, more motivating (a matter of opinion), flexible enough to fit into a version of implementation that works for your lifestyle, and way more fun than the stuffy goal process some of us have come to avoid.

The next step toward developing your goals is to create an Action Plan. The official action plan typically addresses the following:

- Answers the questions of who, what where, why, when and how?
- Addresses possible resistance or barriers to completion
- Identify resources to achieve tasks

Some of these questions are automatically answered due to the nature of this being a personal goal. You may rely on other people or resources, but typically, it can be assumed that most of these actions fall on you unless stated otherwise. You are welcome to be as detailed as you need to suit your personality.

My preference for an action plan is really an organized "To Do" list for specific aspects of my goal. Much like writing your thoughts on paper allows you to build on your thoughts, writing your to do list allows you to focus on the current task, rather than continue to replay in your mind what you still have left undone. The benefits of having an action plan include releasing distraction, organizing chaos, and providing a sense of accomplishment. There is great satisfaction that comes with crossing items off your list. I have suggested in previous chapters to employ list making to see the benefits in your life. The awesome reward that comes with writing to do lists is that you will reap the benefits immediately - instant gratification.

For personal goal purposes, I have included the following in a modified or dirty version of the action plan:

- Major milestones
- Individual milestone task lists
- Plan to monitor and evaluate action plan
- Time commitment to action plan and overall goal

The format of your action plan will look different to suit your organization style. Some people need extensive details laid out like roadmap instructions to help get them from one point to another. This roadmap may involve the entire scope of the goal, or it could be a roadmap for one of the main tasks within your personal goal. When I made the goal to write this book, I made an initial list of major milestones in the book.

My written milestones included writing, editing, publishing, and marketing. I did research and took notes on all aspects as they revealed themselves through my thoughts, but after writing the information down, I returned my focus , energy and efforts on the first task of writing the book. My action plan for the first task of writing took the form of an outline, with a side to do list that I would carry forward from day to day. The tasks I had to work on were organizing headings within chapters and building out the content one piece of the puzzle at a time.

On a smaller scale, I also documented one main goal task I wanted to complete that day while I was journaling. At the end of the day, I would make sure that I had all of the daily tasks done on my list. My to do list carries forward from day to day, and week to week. When it gets messy, I rewrite my to do list and carry forward the items that I have not yet completed. The journal was an extra task master, but it was part of my Miracle Morning. Seeing that I set goals in the morning and verified that I had accomplished them before I went to bed was motivating.

CONSIDER THIS:

A "To do" list allows you to have accountability for what you need to get done, but also allows you to release the distraction of all you have left undone. If life gives you an opportunity to enjoy your time with friends and family – take it! Your to-do list has got you covered. Live life. Enjoy the moments you get to spend with others. Make memories. If you are rigid on the time you spend working toward your personal goal, you may find that you get resistance from others because your loved ones may feel neglected, and you may get burned out because you don't give yourself a break. Rely on your to-do list to have your back when you decide to nurture other aspects of your life.

Below is a very basic action plan including a to-do list and granular level task format that I have used for your reference. There are also a large variety of options available on an internet search or Word templates if you use that program. Please use a format that works best for you, or build your own method using (or not) the suggestions provided. Again, flexible to your liking. Another option is to utilize a digital option in the form of an app for a to do list or action plan. Research a few and test them out. If the phone option works best for you, then use it. There is something gratifying about written calendars and to do lists that I have not experienced with the digital option. However, I cannot say that I have given any apps a fair shot to change my mind. See the following for my written example, which is a cleaned-up version of the action plan format I used to write this book:

Goal: Write a book on finding and developing personal goals

Major goal milestones:

Write (including research)

- Outline
- Chapter headings

Edit

- Who?
- What steps do I need to follow to get to this point?

Publish

- What options are available for publishing?
- What formats will I consider?

Market

- Social Media
- Advertising

(The above section is reviewed periodically and as needed to keep in sync with your ultimate goal – monitor and adjust)

Tasks for writing milestones (To do list or micro functions of your goals):

~~Create a rough book outline~~

~~Research goal statistics~~

~~Develop chapter outline~~

~~Expand chapter 1 content~~

(The above section carries forward from day to day to keep your goal on task)

I shared my version of the action plan in the form of a to do list not because I don't think people know how to make a list, but rather to demonstrate how simple it can be to develop an action plan.

Monitoring and Evaluating
Your Action Plan

Accountability for your action plan helps to ensure you stay on track. Monitoring and evaluating your action plan is critical to staying the course. This can be as simple as marking tasks complete by crossing them off the list so they are still legible. You can use a single strike through like I have above, a check mark to the side, or highlight with colored marker to indicate a task is complete. Using one of these methods ensures you still have notes that you can refer back to when you are working through your development and achievement process. Reviewing your major goal milestones and to-do lists on a regular basis is the best method for ensuring that nothing in your journey gets missed. Make sure that you have defined a plan to monitor and evaluate your action plan.

Time Commitments in Your Action Plan

An action plan is not just a list of tasks you need to complete. You should also have an idea or expectation about the time you will allow to work on your goals. A backup plan for making up time when life presents other opportunities is also critical for success. When I decided to write this book, I knew that my excitement was at risk of becoming a source of stress if I found myself battling in a fight for the time to commit to the work. I knew that if my action plan was rigid and too demanding it could cause arguments at home. So I immediately decided that if there was ever a question about spending time with my boyfriend, my family, or my puppies (they let me know when they need my undivided attention), I would always choose the opportunity to have those moments and make those memories, as opposed to knocking out my to do list. I also know myself well enough that I knew I had the drive and discipline to work on the book whenever I had free moments.

My plan was to commit my writing hours to the time I spent in airports, airplanes, hotels (I often travel for work), early weekend mornings, and evenings that I was home alone. This plan allowed me to keep my schedule free when I had an opportunity to spend time with my family and released me from feeling like I was failing at my goals if I wasn't writing every day. Writing a book is a very big commitment, one would occupy hundreds of hours not only writing, but also developing the content through mental exercises and techniques.

A realistic working plan made at the beginning of the project set the expectation for me and allowed me to share it with my boyfriend who also knew that he was my priority. Since writing every day was never part of the plan initially, I felt good when I met the commitments to write according to my original plan. If I had set the expectation that I had to write every day, I might get discouraged and irritated when the plan didn't work out. Be realistic about your commitments in life. It's unfortunate how unclear and unrealistic expectations can foil your excitement and motivation to achieve your goals. Make a plan to fit your lifestyle and give yourself a break when life throws you other social opportunities.

This plan worked for me. Figure out what works for you and be accountable for your own success - not only in your personal goals, but also in your personal life. Make sure that you consider how other aspects of your life will be affected when constructing your action plan. Commit to only 30 minutes a day if that works for you, knowing that you may have to be flexible on when those 30 minutes might happen someday. Wake up early or squeeze it into your schedule, take action while you are waiting for kids to get done with practice, or wait for their game to start. Also, remember that the time you set aside needs to work with the timing for the tasks on your list. If you need to reach out to people or businesses as part of your tasks on your action plan, you need to plan for time during hours you can reach these resources.

Have fun with your goal journey. Bend, contort and shape the process to fit your lifestyle, motivational style, and basic preferences. One of the biggest issues that have the potential to hinder the journey to our goals is that we think we need to fit our goal setting and achieving into this square peg, when our lives are a distorted star shape. If you like the computer, make a list there. If you like your phone, get the app. If we open up our minds to the possibilities, we open up our opportunity to succeed.

The fun of goal setting starts when we get into the meat and potatoes of the process. When you get to start working on tasks that move you closer to your goal. Remember to document tasks, outcomes from the tasks, and follow-up with an update to your goal detail metrics (SMART details) if anything has changed. And remember to keep using your 6000+ thoughts a day to help you progress through and continue to develop and achieve your goals.

CHAPTER 11

Keeping Your Goals Fresh

The TAP goal development process presented in this book is really basic and sounds easy enough. We are taking super basic practices and using them in a very focused and purposeful manner. The practice of Thinking, Acting (writing), and Processing alone isn't the difficult part of the practice. The biggest challenges we face are those that we face in everything we do in life. The motivation to start and the willingness to continue to the finish. There are so many influencing dynamics in our lives that smother our excitement and motivation to develop, much less reach our goals.

Playing it safe will get you into retirement given that you plan and put that specific goal into action. However, achieving the goal of retirement may not provide you with a feeling of fulfillment, much less happiness in our daily lives before we reach that stage. In chapter 5 we discussed all of the reasons we either don't set goals or we fail to follow-through with the goals we do set. In this chapter we will discuss tools and techniques to keep your goals fresh so you will have the motivation and desire to follow-through with your goals to fruition.

A New Perspective On An Old Goal

There are times when the vision of your goals may become unclear or when you may not feel the excitement for your goals the way you did in the beginning. The 2015 film *The Intern* with Robert DeNiro and Anne Hathaway is a perfect example of losing sight of your goals. Anne Hathaway's character, although extremely successful, has lost her excitement for her life's work due to other situational circumstances.

Robert DeNiro's character is the catalyst she needs to refocus and reevaluate aspects of her life, family, and career that are contributing to her current unrest. Relying on his wisdom from a life full of experience, he offers a new (but old) perspective to Anne's character that provides the insight and guidance she needs to navigate her challenges and reset her perspective on her goals.

Now, I wish we could all have a side kick like Robert DeNiro. I would happily perch up on a bed with him and watch old movies any day! However, there are other techniques and resources that can help you to refocus. If it helps to get more excited about practicing these tools and techniques, we can think of them as our pseudo Robert DeNiro. These options include, but are definitely not limited to:

- Motivational or educational YouTube videos
- An abundance of podcasts
- Endless books
- Exercise
- A day, weekend, or week of relaxation to help you reset
- Deep or rhythmic breathing
- Tapping
- Meditation (Ugh!)
- Thought Action Process to get a new perspective
- Research

Some of these tools and techniques are briefly discussed in this book, others are only mentioned in the above list. Use your resources (internet, books, etc.) to discover more about any of these pseudo-Robert DeNiro options to help you through challenges in life. I will expand specifically on research, recognizing signs that guide you on the right path, and recognizing resistance vs challenges, as these aspects can largely affect the outcomes (or lack of outcomes) of our goals. These are practices we use and see every day, so we may think we are experts. However, as with anything in life, complacency leads to inefficient practices and unintended lack of awareness. Keep an open mind and be willing to refresh your practices.

Research

Research is a great way to refresh your goals. No matter what goals you are working on (personal, career, work, resolutions, or life path) research will provide information, direction, and perspective. That is as long as you are open to new information. When seeking new information, try to release your grip on what you think you know as your brain will try to automatically adjust the new information to assimilate it with old information, which ineffectively just gets you the same results you've gotten previously. Do your research with the intent of discovery. To really understand where your challenges are originating, you need to be willing to admit that your perception may be incomplete, wrong, or misguided. If you are sensitive to constructive criticism, there is a high likelihood that you will be blind to the answer that is hindering your progress. Effective research is done with an open mind, a desire to succeed, and a willingness to accept and integrate new information.

When researching for a personal goal, I make sure that I am "searching wide". If you haven't noticed, when you type in a key search, the internet provides context that matches the tone of your search term. If you are looking to develop a new product or method that is not already available, you will want to take a step back and research from a 30,000-foot view. For instance, if you dislike the current options available for a duvet cover and are searching "design options for duvet cover", those exact words bring up more information that you already know about current duvet covers.

Those are good words to type in if you are looking for options that are already available on the market. If you are looking to design a new option, you might take a step back and search "how to sew a comforter", you can review sewing instructions step-by-step and consider how to adjust these instructions to determine a solution for the issue you are trying to solve. There are a million different ways you can search, but a narrow search term will bring you expected results. When searching widely, you are not necessarily searching for terms that directly relate to your product or method.

Using the search wide method will help original ideas to start flowing while you research and consider your product materials, design, marketing, and alternative products. Additionally, research also helps if you are having trouble collaborating with others, procrastinating, finding motivation, or any other aspect that is hindering the progress toward your goal. Even though this task takes time, it will likely help you to reach your goal faster than if you continue with the status quo of procrastination and deflated motivation.

The benefit of open-minded research is that we are continually taking in information that challenges the truths we hold. By doing this, we inwardly acknowledge that the beliefs we hold are our limiting factor and we are able to release these beliefs. If you don't know how to research with an open mind, try researching ideas that challenge your way of thinking. Truly read and consider alternative beliefs to get the benefit of increased knowledge and alternative perspectives.

Keep in mind that the goal of this exercise is not to prove yourself wrong, it is to evolve and grow in your knowledge. This alternative perspective helps us get our creative juices flowing and helps us to also evolve our thoughts so we can achieve and create more. The moral of this discussion on research is that you can't expect to implement research that only supports your current way of thinking – you should want to research to get to the information that will help you succeed at achieving your goals. If you are committed to creating the best outcome for your goals, you will keep your goals fresh by researching and making changes to your goal and your person continuously.

Confirmation

It's always comforting to have confirmation that you are on the right path. These moments of confirmation help to refresh your motivation to continue on your path to success. Hearing stories about others stepping outside of their comfort zones to achieve greatness is motivating for me. On my own path I battled the thoughts of doubt that tried to creep in and sabotage my journey. When your goals are not feeling fresh and exciting, these limiting thoughts have a greater opportunity to take hold.

I kept following the path that was opening up to me throughout my goal journey. The confirmation and motivational stories that I needed to continue toward my goal of writing this book became too obvious for me to quit on myself. They were the moments that propelled me forward to continue creating and evolving to reach the end product. I want to share with you some of the experiences that helped me in my journey to keep writing. The goal is to get you to recognize the stories and signs that will hopefully motivate you to keep going as well. These simple stories that act as prompts could easily be dismissed if you aren't aware and don't appreciate their value.

Inspirational Stories

As I was just starting this journey - still reading The Miracle Morning, but already working on this book – my mother was driving back home to Minnesota from visiting a friend in Texas. When she was about an hour and a half from a junction where she could continue to drive home or turn to see me in Denver, she called to see if we were up for an impromptu visit from her. Yes please! She ended up staying for a week. That week was full of great conversation, walks through Morse Park and Crown Hill, and a few cocktails by the fire.

At the time, my parents were just going through the process of selling their business that she and my father had started in 1984. The business was their fourth child and such a large part of my family. They had started the business with a $6000 loan that they had used to buy a van and some material. My dad recalls how terrified he was because he did not know how they were going to pay the "couple hundred dollar a month" loan payment, but decided to let my mother, his finance partner, worry about making the payment. He would focus on getting and doing the electrical work.

The inspirational part of this story that I needed to hear at the time was that big decisions come with an inherent fear. This fear could have held my father back, but by choosing to take the risk he achieved success. He was making $6 an hour as an electrician back then and was being prompted by my Grandpa Jerry (my mother's father) and my mother to start his own business. He had three children and a wife to provide for, and the decision had to be incredibly stressful, and fear multiplied by infinity. But he and my mother took the leap and defeated fear. The payoff was a life of hard work, a thriving business, and respect for and from his employees whom he regarded as family.

At a time when I needed to have the motivation to take a risk myself, I was reminded that I had a full-time job, no children's well-being at risk, and the financial risk I was taking (the road to publishing and advertising is the expensive part) would be minimal in comparison to the risk they took all those years ago. I really had no excuse not to go for it!

Signs

Similar to the motivational effect of an inspirational story, signs from God and the universe provide the comforting feeling you get in knowing that you are on the right path. These signs are revealed in our awareness and are a result of taking action. At the time I was writing this book I received several signs that granted me the motivation to keep going. The first sign that got everything rolling was that everything from the first day flowed. I was putting forth a lot of time and energy, but the work was fun and ideas presented themselves allowing me to move forward quickly.

In that single morning I realized through The Miracle Morning process that I had no goals, I researched to determine how to discover my goals, decided to write a book due to lack of guidance, and figured out a method to discover my goals. Using the process I discovered that morning, I continued to write this book day after day, week after week. I wasn't struggling to find the motivation or the content on which to write, I just implemented what I had discovered. I did have the major challenge of being limited on time, as I have a very busy full-time job, a boyfriend, and three dogs that I want to spend my extra time enjoying. Given this time challenge, I still found plenty of time to write almost every day.

The second sign came in confirmation for a second goal of mine. The same day I decided to write a book, I also had decided to work toward a second goal that also appeared through TAPping into my thoughts. I had ideas for a comforter cover that I had been contemplating for several years which had resurfaced that morning. I know you are not supposed to have too many goals at one time, but the timing just seemed right. It was moving at a slower pace than the book, but the project was still moving forward and the signs were apparent that I needed to keep this goal as well. I don't watch television very often, but when I do it is usually Netflix in the evening with my boyfriend before bed.

This particular day, I was taking a water break from my workday and my boyfriend had Ellen on TV (he cannot work without background noise). I walked in as she was interviewing a new author, Ellen Bennett. Ellen Bennett had just released a book on her journey to establishing her apron business. This could not have been a closer situation to the one I was currently exploring, and seeing this particular clip on Ellen was surely a divine message that I was on the right path. The only snippet of Ellen I had watched in over a year was providing direct guidance in the life I was living and the goals I was trying to achieve. For all of you Ellen lovers out there, I think she is great and would watch every day if I had the time. But as it is, I love my job more, which is a good thing!

I cannot end this section without talking about this third additional sign – or omen. The sign confirms a lesson I learned about reading books that come suggested by others. I read every day as part of my Miracle Morning – and sometimes more.

I do love getting book suggestions from people on content they have enjoyed, but believe that you will only find as much enjoyment and value in a particular book when the topic is relevant to your current life scenario. If the book is not relevant you will not appreciate the message in the book. I had heard about the book *The Alchemist* by Paulo Coelho a while back, and it had been in my queue to read. However, while I was waiting for my book by Ellen Bennett to show up, I decided to finally read *The Alchemist*.

At a time where I was receiving so many signals that I was on the right path, comes a book that details a boy's life that is guided by recognizing signs from the universe as omens and providing direction to a relatively lost soul looking for his personal goal. This was the absolute best time for me to read that specific book. I know I would have enjoyed the book either way, but would not have appreciated the true value had I not read it at this exact point in my life. You don't need to force things – even reading books. If you focus on taking action, the right resources will present themselves at the right time. This will help you to follow your own path in your own time. The key is to always be taking action – and if writing is the action you take, it will have more benefits than you realize. Lack of action leads to lack of results.

Three very evident signs in a very short amount of time. The nearly effortless flow of information and ideas, the presentation of a book that would be helpful in one goal, and a message in a book that made evident the signs I was identifying were truly meant for confirmation. The signs were a gift and were what I needed to push forward in my goal journeys.

A Word on Resistance

Have you ever had those days where nothing seems to go your way and it appears that the whole universe is working against you? That is not how God, the universe, or any other spiritual presence works. In the words of Paulo Coelho in *The Alchemist*, "when you want something, all the universe conspires in helping you to achieve it". I truly believe these words. When you are on the right path, and when you realize your true passion, goals, meaning - or however you want to refer to it - God will put signs of confirmation in your path that will help to accelerate you in your journey. On the contrary, if you are living a life that is not meant for you – be it striving for others people's goals and expectations, taking the path you see as the easy way, or a path of ill intent – the world will keep giving you challenges to redirect you. This doesn't necessarily mean that you need to change your path entirely (unless you have ill intent), but rather that you may need a new perspective or a new strategy.

Don't mistaken challenges for unhappiness. Only you can find happiness within you. If you haven't figured out that your unhappiness is preventing you from living your life, then you are unlikely to be available to enjoy all of the gifts that the world has given you. When you are unhappy, you need to determine whether that unhappiness is truly a product of your situation (i.e., abusive or disrespectful relationship) or a product of your own choosing (i.e. anger and victim mentality). Either way, until you leave the unhappy situation or quit choosing to be unhappy, you will be blinded to the doors of the worlds' gifts and happiness.

Don't mistaken challenges for resistance. Challenges are inevitable. They provide an opportunity to overcome. Resistance is opposition to what you are trying to achieve. If every direction of your turn you are in turns receiving a "no", you need a refresh. A new perspective. A new angle. A new strategy. If you are still facing opposition, turn back to Chapter 8 on brainstorming and start the process over again. Your thoughts will help you to determine if this is not the right time for this personal goal, or if you have been going at it all wrong, as well as give you direction for a new path or perspective.

Life's challenges are not a curse or punishment for something you have done or not done. Challenges are God's gift to us – a gift that presents opportunities to learn, grow and get a new perspective. It is from these opportunities that we gain knowledge, compassion, and the fulfillment that can be so hard to find. The ability to overcome challenges is a great strength. A strength that everyone of us has the capability to employ in our lives, but not everyone has the tenacity to discover within themselves due to perspective, or the lack thereof. Evaluate your responses as you journey through challenges. If you see yourself and respond as a victim of circumstances, you need to change your view and your tactics.

Many people with healthy attitudes and successful lives have come from adverse pasts. An amazing example of overcoming challenges is Dave Pelzer, the author of *The Child Called "It"* series. As a boy he was horrifically abused by his mother. He could have chosen to let the abuse kill him (some of his experiences surely could have), or he could have grown up to be an abusive alcoholic and let the cycle continue the way his mother did. At 7 he chose to overcome and live. He saw living as a daily challenge to conquer at an age when most of us were still being put to bed by our parents. He is now the author of more than 10 books. His story is one of many amazing lives that so easily could have ended in tragedy, but his will to live is incredibly inspiring. When you observe the magnitude of the challenges he encountered, it puts our own daily life's challenges into a whole new perspective. The challenges we let defeat us are ultimately excuses, as many times they would be easily overcome. Constantly seeking a new perspective over feelings of defeat will help you to keep your goals fresh and prevent the outcome of your goal from being stale.

What I hope you get from this information is the comfort of knowing that God, or the universe, or whatever spiritual being you credit for guiding you, has your back. If you listen and watch, you too will receive messages from the universe to help you keep your life and goals on track, and possibly even give guidance on which road to travel. Put the need to control your life aside, be open to receiving these messages, and have the willingness to act on them.

Keep it Relevant

You may have developed a goal or are working on something that brings you fulfillment right now, but purpose and fulfillment will evolve as your life evolves. The same idea or the same angle will not remain motivating and inspiring throughout your entire life – probably not even through an entire year. This is the essence of keeping it fresh. Relevance of a goal in your life will change, so your goals will need to evolve as you evolve. Resistance will fade when your goals are relevant in your life. The details and direction of your goals will change as you evolve or achieve milestones.

This is the benefit of continually TAP(ping) into your thoughts throughout the lifecycle of your goals. Using your thoughts to guide the direction of your goals will keep your goals relevant and fresh. If you are thinking about it, you can be comfortable considering that it is relevant in your life at this stage. Discovering, developing and achieving your goals should be fun. You can carry that fun and fulfillment throughout your life by TAP(ping) into your thoughts and ideas throughout your life. Don't stop TAP(ping) into your thoughts when you identify a goal. And don't take just one personal goal journey. Look forward to a life of journeys and a life of using your thoughts to guide you and keep your ideas, goals, and life fresh.

Do the work. Do the work to develop your goals. Do the work to keep yourself motivated and on track for your goals. A world of benefits for doing so is waiting for you. In the next chapter we will discuss these benefits to understand why putting in the work for setting and achieving goals is worth it.

CHAPTER 12

An Abundance of Benefits

We have let ourselves believe that we are too busy to do anything other than live our lives the way we have been. We cannot fit another task into our busy days. From sunup to sundown, every moment is accounted for. Except for the moments when we get to take a breath. Those rare moments where we get to watch tv or browse our phones, but that is sacred untouchable "me time". We are stuck in the lie that those moments help us to relax and reset so we can make it through another day.

Does this sound familiar? Is this the narrative you tell yourself and everyone else? Before you start setting and achieving goals, we need to first change the narrative we cling to, so we can change our perspective and our beliefs. The benefits will not only affect how successful you are at setting and achieving goals but will better your entire life in remarkable ways. When you choose to change your life, you will see how the habits of social media and television are more draining than restoring. You're welcome.

I was the one who believed the previous narrative. I got lucky because when I realized my goal, I was so excited and motivated that the choice between television, social media, and other wasted phone time was not even a question. When I had "free time" my attention immediately went to writing this book. For those who don't have a goal in mind and have not worked through the process to identify a goal, you may have to work on changing your belief about your time before you are willing to do the work. The great news is that once you do the work to change your narrative, the profound effect of redirecting your focus to something constructive has wonderful side effects that can be appreciated immediately. You may find yourself enjoying the same benefits, or others of which I may not yet be aware. The following are some of the wonderful benefits that are waiting for you on the other side.

Increased Focus

The mundane repetitiveness of our everyday lives reduces our attention. We don't have to think much about the things we do every day because they are habits and have been referred to in this book as living on autopilot. I sometimes find that I don't remember doing a task because I am paying such little attention to my actions and getting lost in my thoughts. Changing up the thought process and viewing our daily tasks from a different angle increases focus and energy. When you change your angle, you are automatically required to increase your focus because you are no longer doing the same task in the same way. And when you change your routine, the inherent effect on your life is increased energy because you have escaped the mundane.

I found that I could get more work done in a shorter amount of time from this increased focused. I now understand the essence of the quote from Benjamin Franklin "If you want something done, ask a busy person". When I got busy with tasks that were fueling me and no longer wasting my time on activities that drain me, my focus increased to be incredibly more efficient.

CONSIDER THIS:

Take something you do every day and research a better way to get that task done. For instance, putting away laundry. You may battle with limited space and hate putting away laundry because you are constantly cramming your clothes into the space to make it all fit. Instead of hating the task and doing things the way you have always done it, research what you can do to make it better. Suggestions like getting rid of old items, storing out-of-season clothing in a different space, or creative suggestions for folding, hanging and organizing your clothes will train your brain to consider better alternatives. These suggestions help you to focus on the possibilities and realize there are other areas of your life you can focus on to improve as well. Get your brain thinking in a different manner and your focus will help you find the answers for which you didn't even know you needed to make improvements in your daily habits.

Increased Energy

A polished and practiced autopilot mode does not equal energy. I consider one of the best aspects about autopilot is the opportunity to think and create, but most of us don't do that either. Think about the energy you feel when you are excited about something – vacation, a new opportunity, and an upcoming event that you are invited to attend. If you take a minute to really think about yourself in those situations you can feel that energy coursing through your body.

The journey to your personal goals can give you that same surge of energy. Adding variety and a change in your everyday activities has the same effect. Goals are an awesome ingredient that can provide this variety in your days. If you set a goal and don't feel that energy, then you are working against the system. Find a new goal or a new perspective on your goal. One that makes you feel the energy. That energy sticks with us and seeps into the other aspects of our lives. We have more energy for life in general when we are excited about goals, habits and events in our lives we are working toward. If you are on autopilot you may need to change your routine and way of thinking to find your energy.

CONSIDER THIS:

Try finding one small goal you have been wanting to work toward. This may be in the form of a beaten path/expectation goal, work goal, career goal, resolution, or personal goal. It might just be

> *researching education options, asking your boss about opportunities to get more experience or broaden your work scope, losing weight, improving health, or researching and making an action list for a personal goal you have been considering. Focus on the feeling you have while you consider the possibilities that these opportunities may bring. Use that energy you feel as momentum to propel you through your journey.*

Increased Happiness and Excitement

We get bored. It happens. Allowing ourselves to stay bored gives us time to think about ourselves and everything that is wrong with us. Everything that could stand improvement. And then we somehow start to believe that others see these same things in us. Not only do they see these same faults, but they also think about our faults constantly as we do. In reality they absolutely do not. A bored mind will let you believe that you are the center of everyone else's thoughts and concerns. But really either they are thinking about their own busy life, or they are getting bogged down themselves with these same disruptive and toxic thoughts. Goal setting gets you out of your own head. It gives you something to focus on other than the untruths our bored mind keeps telling us. When you focus on the possibilities, your thoughts are externalized, and your mind goes to work for you – not against you.

The variety in your days also helps to add some spice to your life. There is excitement in finding out what is coming next. That excitement doesn't stop at your goals alone, it stays with you in anticipation of your every day. When you set personal goals and work toward achieving them, no two days are the same. Your days change incrementally while you gather information from research or complete tasks toward your goals. When you achieve tasks, it will affect and change the angle of the goal.

Remember that goals are not straight lines, which helps you adjust your focus on your path. Your personal goals adjust when you gather information or realize that the trajectory of the goal is affected by the completion of a task. The benefit of this is that the momentum doesn't allow boredom to set in. The changing landscape allows you to keep that smile on your face and excitement in your life.

I have been lucky to only experience depression for 2 weeks of my life. The onset was a result of side effects from medication. It was the longest, most miserable 2 weeks I can recall. I am very sensitive to depression because it does run in my family. I am not claiming to have answers or really understand the depths of this horrible mental disease. I simply stopped taking the medication and it went away. What it did give me was compassion for people with this disease, and a wish for everyone to find a cure that works for them.

I know sometimes it is a chemical thing that only drugs can cure. I would be interested to know if distractions and busyness would help to get out of your mind to alleviate some of the intensity? If somehow a shift in focus would provide a reprieve from some of those moments and increase happiness. A quote that really resonated with me from the book *Awareness* by Anthony De Mello, is "you are never so centered on yourself when you are depressed, and you are never so ready to forget yourself as when you are happy." Rationalizing this theory makes me believe that if we have a distraction, especially one that we are excited about – that distraction can remove us from thinking about ourselves and put something else in the spotlight of our minds.

CONSIDER THIS:

We are so critical of ourselves and we have a high tendency to think we know how other people perceive us. I have good news! Other people are also focused on themselves. And although they may criticize others, those who criticize are typically much more critical of themselves – a double negative for double unhappiness. Give yourself a break and allow yourself to be human. Your quirks make you unique. Love your quirks!

Increased Productivity

When I initially started to write a book, there was a part of me that worried about the perception my boss might have in regard to the amount of time it takes to write a book, and the amount of time I spend at work. To prevent my work efficiency from suffering and the perception that I was working more on my book than on work, I drew a line in the sand on the time I would spend writing. Taking my own advice in the previous chapters, I allowed myself to jot down notes if something occurred to me during work hours.

Other than basic notes, I only allowed myself to work on the book outside of business hours in the mornings, nights, and weekends. This required that I become more productive at work tasks during business hours Monday through Friday. I was in complete amazement about how much more efficient I became when I had the motivation of getting to work on my goal after work.

Work tasks also became more fun because I started to look at them from a different perspective. I started to get more creative and interested in how I could make a bigger impact in my role and looked into ways I could expand my scope of responsibilities. Not only did I become more productive at work, I became more beneficial in my role because I was excited to think out of the box and view my work goals in a different light. Through this experience I realized that you can be a really good employee by getting your work done in a timely, efficient, and correct manner, or you can be a great employee by changing your angle to view things from a perspective that you had never before considered. The catalyst for me to be more productive was to bring excitement back to my days by adding personal goals. A win for me, and a win for my company and career.

CONSIDER THIS:

The way you view things is only an opinion. It's not fact. Learn something new. Look at something from someone else's point of view. Learn a new way to do something. If it's not better than the way you are, you can go back informed. Keep looking for ways to improve. There is no telling what amazing things you will find that will accelerate your life when you consider the possibilities!

Being Present/Awareness

This was by far the most amazing transformation in my journey towards my goal. I was one of those people who would have swore that I only spent a half-hour a day on my phone looking at social media. I only knew that I spent more time on my phone because I dove into the details on the screen time phone app, which told me that I was spending about 6 hours on my phone – and about half of that was social media. I always chalked my high phone usage to the GPS app, reading books, listening to audio books, listening to podcasts, on calls for work, or looking at work email. Social media was the least of my time spent on my phone. Right. I am embarrassed to say how much time I was wasting, which on average was at least half of my overall phone time.

Fast forward only weeks to the time that I started working on personal goals. Without even trying, my phone time dropped by three hours! And less than 1 hour of that time was spread amongst social media platforms (which means I still had some time to shave). Fast forward by a couple more weeks after I watched the Netflix documentary on social media and that number has now dropped to under 10 minutes. Part of this change did have to do with the impact of the documentary, but mostly was due to increased time working on my goals. It's amazing how much you can achieve when you become aware of the time suck of social media.

Having purpose in my personal life provided the inherent benefit of awareness. Awareness of the things that are really important. I don't need to remind myself not to check my phone – I have gotten really good at forgetting. I am too busy doing other things that I want to be doing, things that provide value and substance to my life.

Social media has become a place to share the perception you want others to have of your life. My boyfriend's father says that pictures are a reminder of what you could have been doing if you weren't busy taking pictures. Translate that into today's world where social media has become a reminder of all the things you did between checking and updating your social media. Without additional effort or awareness of what I was doing, personal goal setting made me become aware and present with my family and friends. I genuinely enjoy the company of those around me and would rather spend time enjoying them than being lured into a fruitless scroll for fulfillment and gratification. I now really listen to others when they speak. I hear what they are saying and don't pretend to listen. I get so much more out of life than I ever appreciated when I was on autopilot.

CONSIDER THIS:

Look at your screen time and a breakdown of the activity on your phone. Now consider the value you have gotten from the time you have spent on each app. After evaluating this information, do you feel good about the time you spent on your phone? Remember that every minute you are on your phone, you are not living. You are not spending time with your partner, you are not spending time with your kids, you are not working on you to improve your life for you and that of your family. Choose wisely because you don't get this wasted time back.

Saving Money

This was a totally unexpected advantage of goal setting, but a welcome one. There is an array of psychological reasons people spend money, which include a lack of fulfillment, competition, keeping up with the Jones's, celebration, efforts to thwart negative emotions, and boredom. The wonderful effect of goal setting is that it takes the focus off of what might be missing in your life, and highlights your abilities and the endless possibilities that might come from your untapped potential. When you are focusing on positive and engaging projects, the result ends up being a redirection of your attention from negative emotions to an excitement that creates a wonderful feeling of fulfillment. Like magic, the need for external gratification to fill a void is gone.

CONSIDER THIS:

If the need to spend less money is an issue you need to address in your life, try this trick. Make a rule that anything you are going to buy you need to sit on for 2 days. If you still feel you need the item in two days, you can consider buying it at that time. Our need for instant gratification can be replaced by focusing our attention on other motivating projects. When I implement this practice, I tend to forget that I needed the item in the first place.

End Mindless Grazing

When we are bored or emotional, we tend to head to the kitchen (that is if we aren't out shopping). We eat our feelings. When we are busy, no matter the reason, we forget about grazing because we are focused on something else. We don't need to fill moments with mindless action because we are mentally and physically busy. Who needs external gratification when you are already feeling fulfilled? It's an unintended benefit, but awesome nonetheless.

You will notice that many of these benefits influence the other benefits. If you go back to Chapter 5, you will notice that the same is true for sabotage behaviors. If you practice behaviors in one chapter, the other behaviors in that same chapter will follow. The fact is that good thoughts and feelings bring on more good thoughts and feelings. The same is true for negative feelings. Choose to live in the benefit chapter, not the sabotage chapter. The common theme of these benefits is that having something productive and fun to focus on creates a better internal environment.

Mental health in the form of fulfillment, satisfaction, happiness, focus, and energy (to name a few) are a side effect of focusing your thoughts and energy outward. If we don't have something external to keep our minds busy, we start to focus too much on ourselves and suddenly, somehow, we start to believe that we are not enough. The truth is that the focus we put on ourselves is not enough – we need more than ourselves to focus on. As human beings we need something more, but we have let settling for good enough be okay. Let's not do that anymore. Let's put our time and energy into something awesome. Let's create an amazing life of possibilities for ourselves and stop waiting on someone or something else to do that for us.

Are these awesome benefits of personal goal setting amazing enough that you realize you need to make time for personal goals in your life? Evaluate your life. Evaluate where you spend your time. Evaluate your choices. If you are sitting in the car or in the bleachers waiting for your kids to finish practice or start their game, choose to spend that waiting time doing something productive. All it takes is to choose to redirect 30 minutes, an hour -

whatever you can spare - to work on a goal that could change your life.

CHAPTER 13

Conclusion – Where To Next?

You are here. You have made it to the last chapter. Now is the moment of truth. Now is the moment that you decide how you will proceed with your life. You have read the book and have either enjoyed it and found it of value, found it completely useless in your life, or somewhere on the spectrum in between. The value is a reflection of the relevance of the material at this particular point in your life. Similarly, the outcome of reading this book is completely reliant on how you implement this theory and these tools in your life. The options you have moving forward include:

1. Put the title on a mental list in a category of usefulness you found the book to provide, be able to say you read the book, possibly

provide a review of the book online prompting others to read it, or not waste their time, and move on as if you never read it.

2. Play around with the suggestions shared in the book, start taking notes, and see where it leads. These tools and suggestions that you implement now may follow you to a time in your life when personal goals are more relevant, and you will have the knowledge in your back pocket when an opportunity presents itself.

3. The last option is to jump in. See where the journey takes you. TAP into the goldmine that is your brain to create goals that can elevate your life.

The truth is that making a long-term change to your habits, or implementing new but long-lasting strategies to improve your life, is relatively uncommon. Many start a journey with good intentions, only to give up when the new plan does not fit easily into their lives. The proposed strategy is not one that will provide you with amazing results without putting in the work. The event of starting new habits or new endeavors is the miraculous result of the collision of information, at the same time as your brain is open to receiving the information, at the same time as you have the motivation to make the change. I have referred to this idea previously as an "aha moment".

The "aha moment" coupled with the relevance of information at the time it is presented explains why one person can read a book and think it is fantastic, while another's review is mediocre at best. The value or relevance of your current life experiences and focus is directly related to the value and interest a topic has for you. Relevance is also the reason that I recommend the books I have referred to with a caveat of putting them on your list to be read when the title or topic pops out at you. Craig Beck suggests that readers don't need to recommend his book to anyone – if a person needs it, they will find it. Although I understand why he makes this statement, I love getting recommendations of books from people – I just recognize that I need to put it on the list and read it when it is relevant to me. *The Alchemist* was on my list and was available to me when I needed to recognize the signals the universe was sending me. I became aware of *Dream First, Details Later* when I was working on a relevant goal, it is now on my list to read but is delayed in being sent to me. I take this as a sign from the universe that I am not yet meant to read the book. I am confident that the book will be available to me when I am meant to read it, as right now I may not take away the full value of the book. I accredit this to the relevance of the book not being in the same place as the progress of my goal so I will likely miss much of the intended message.

Another important consideration when trying to make improvements or changes in your life is that a message delivered is not the same as a message received. You are only open to receive information that fits with your current thinking and your beliefs. Psychologist Ralph Lewis states that beliefs are templates for efficient learning and that we use our beliefs to absorb and filter massive amounts of information we process daily. The message you receive is influenced by your beliefs.

Two people can read the same article, hear the same presentation, or watch the same event and walk away with different perceptions of a message. Although our beliefs are supposed to be beneficial in helping us, they can equally deter us from moving forward or accepting new information because it does not fit with our current belief system. The important take away is that our beliefs ARE NOT facts. Our beliefs are an assimilation of information to the experiences and information we hold to be true.

If you are ever contemplating what you are holding onto is fact or belief, it is advised that you regard your thoughts as a belief and allow for additional information to become better informed. If you really want to change your life and strive for your goals, know that you will increase your chances for success by being open to new ideas and new information and not commit yourself to a belief. Tying yourself and your goals to your beliefs will automatically put limitations on your possibilities. Choose to be limitless.

Key Takeaways

Your reading is coming to an end, but your journey is hopefully just beginning. As a bon voyage to help you with a successful start to your journey, let's review the lessons learned and key takeaways found throughout this book.

- You are never too busy to set goals. Put yourself and your family first by choosing to prioritize *you* in your life.

- You are never too old to set goals. Retirement is as great a time as any to start goal setting as you are likely to find yourself with an abundance of time.

- Don't live on autopilot. If you take nothing else from this book, at the very least change up your routine, your habits, and your sources of information to help you grow and live a life where you are aware of your choices and beliefs. Live in awareness.

- There are 5 basic types of goals – personal goals are the one type of goal that will help you to elevate your life to a level you thought you could only imagine – a life most others are not living.

- Personal goals provide fulfillment that you are looking for and can't find it in daily life, expectations goals, or when scrolling social media.

- You are already on the path to success just by considering personal goal setting. Most American's don't take the time to set goals, even though goal setting is associated with increased success, fulfillment, and happiness.

- Dirty goals help to fit the process of discovering, developing, and achieving your personal goals into your life and motivation style. Following conventional rules makes the process stuffy and unmotivating for some.

- Stop self-sabotaging behaviors. Self-sabotaging behaviors bring on more negative behaviors, emotions, and feelings. Give yourself a break and celebrate you.
- It's so incredibly worth repeating – limit (or better yet just get off) social media. There are very limited benefits from the time you spend scrolling.
- Don't wait until you have all of the details of the goal to take action. Take action to figure out your goals and gather details while you are feeling excited and motivated.
- Plan to brainstorm while you are doing mindless tasks such as exercising or stuffing envelopes. But be prepared to take notes of great ideas that can come at any time.
- Always have some method available to write your thoughts.
- Write your thoughts immediately so you don't lose them.
- Writing your thoughts also helps you to develop and grow additional thoughts as your mind is allowed to let go of the initial

thought since you now have it documented. This is also referred to as the Zeigarnik Effect.

- Don't limit yourself with your beliefs that ideas are unrealistic or impossible. Learn to consider the possibilities instead.
- Get in the habit of writing a to do list. It's good evidence as to the value of writing thoughts down, but it also makes you more focused and more efficient as you are not constantly considering everything you have left undone.
- Observation of your thoughts + writing your thoughts = Effective brainstorming
- TAP into your goals using the Thought Action Process

  o T(hought) - Data mine your thoughts
  o A(ction) - Write your thoughts on paper or equivalent
  o P(rocess) - Advance or Archive
  o T - Use your continued thoughts to build on that single idea
  o A - Write your thoughts and research on paper or equivalent
  o P - Advance or Archive

o   T - Use a collection of thoughts to develop a goal
o   A - Write your goal on paper
o   P - Develop a fluid action plan

- An action plan allows you to jot down the major steps to achieving your goal, which can then be used to create to-do lists for each of these major steps. You can make the plan as simple or elaborate as you need to organize your journey.

- Always continue to research. When we think we have it figured out, we get introduced to an entirely new perspective that changes our understanding. Keep your eyes and ears open for information that will evolve and increase our understanding.

- A new perspective can reignite our passion for our goals.

- If you pay attention, God and the universe will give you confirmation that you are on the right path. If you are continually running into roadblocks and cannot seem to gain traction, you may need a new perspective, or the timing/relevance for your goal may be off.

- Benefits of personal goal setting include increased focus, increased energy, increased happiness, increased productivity, allowing you to be present in life, among many others.

Always Be Learning

If you look at research that is conducted on any subject in any industry, you will see that all research studies are conducted by "experts" in the field. It is not a novice who would like to learn more about the topic conducting the research. The purpose of research is to advance knowledge about a particular subject. Although these people are experts in their fields, it is well known and understood that there is always more to be learned and always a different angle to look at a topic. How many times throughout the years do we hear conflicting results about the benefits and dangers of caffeine or fatty foods. These two specific food items seem to be very newsworthy. One day they are reporting the health benefits, the next day we are being told they are the cause for our health problems. Research and continual learning give us a new perspective. There is not a single thought, perception, or belief you have that cannot be contradicted or proven otherwise by a different perspective that new information provides. Tying yourself to a belief and committing to that small bit of information as fact is limiting to you and leaves you uninformed.

This book is no different. I have shared with you my journey and my discovery in the hopes that it will be as beneficial to you as it was to me. I'm not suggesting that I have stumbled upon and provided the only way to identify and develop your goals, or that I have the process of developing and achieving goals all figured out. I am always wanting to learn what works for other people on this topic. That being said, I would love to hear your ideas and experiences about discovering your goals. If you have a great idea or have been on a life changing journey while discovering your goals, please share! I would love to hear from you on Instagram and twitter – so please share at #dirtygoaljourney or at AlynMitlyng.com. If we are not always learning and growing, we risk losing opportunity and not living up to our full potential.

I hope that this information has been received with an open mind and collided with a desire to improve your life and gain fulfillment. Whether you embark on a Dirty Goal journey, or you find another method that works for you, I hope you find an experience that delivers your "aha moment" the way I conveniently experienced mine. This moment cannot be forced, but when you experience it, jump on it and ride the wave that it creates. The impact on your life could be monumental.

WORKS CONSULTED AND HONORABLE MENTION

A great big "Thank You" to all of the people, programs, and research sources that have added value to my life and helped to shape the content of this book.

Bargatze, N. "The Greatest Average American." (2021). Netflix.

Beck, C. (2016). The Secret Law of Attraction. Author's Republic.

Bennett, E.M. (2021). Dream First Detials Later. Portfolio.

Calabrese, A. "21 Day Fix." Beachbody. Beachbody On Demand - Streaming Beachbody Workouts Anytime Anywhere - Beachbody.com

Calabrese, A. "9 Week Control Freak." Beachbody. Beachbody On Demand - Streaming

Beachbody Workouts Anytime Anywhere - Beachbody.com

Collins, Bryan. "10 Effective Life Hacks for Work." *Forbes*, Forbes Magazine, 21 Nov. 2019, www.forbes.com/sites/bryancollinseurope/201 9/11/21/10-effective-life-hacks-for-work/?sh=67c204aa1f4b.

Coombe, D, et al. "The Social Dilemma." (2020). Netflix.

de Mello, A. (2000). *Awareness*. Bantam Doubleday Dell.

Diamond, D. *Just 8% of people achieve their New Year's Resolutions. Here's how they do it.* (2013). Forbes. https://www.forbes.com/sites/dandiamond/20 13/01/01/just-8-of-people-achieve-their-new-years-resolutions-heres-how-they-did-it/?sh=61dff048596b.

Elrod, H. (2018). *The miracle morning: The not-so-obvious Secret guaranteed to transform your life before 8am.* Hal Elrod International, Inc.

Gardner, S., & Albee, D. "Study focuses on strategies for achieving goals, resolutions" (2015). Press Releases. 266. https://scholar.dominican.edu/news-releases/266

Harvard Health. "What Causes Depression?" *Harvard Health* (2019), www.health.harvard.edu/mind-and-mood/what-causes-depression.

Hathaway, Anne, Suzanne Farwell, Nancy Meyers, Niro R. De, Linda Lavin, and Rene Russo. The Intern. 2016.

Hill, N. (2007). Think and Grow Rich. Jeremy P. Tarcher.

Lewis, R. What Actually Is a Belief? And Why Is It So Hard to Change? (2018) Psychology Today. https://www.psychologytoday.com/us/blog/finding-purpose/201810/what-actually-is-belief-and-why-is-it-so-hard-change.

Mazzello, Joseph, Oliver Platt, Ian M. Smith, and Ashley Judd. Simon Birch. Place of publication not identified: Hollywood Pictures Home Video, 1999.

Murdock, Jason. "Humans Have More than 6,000 Thoughts per Day, Psychologists Discover." (2020). Newsweek, www.newsweek.com/humans-6000-thoughts-every-day-1517963.

Norcross, J C, and D J Vangarelli. "The resolution solution: longitudinal examination of New Year's change attempts." Journal of Substance Abuse vol. 1,2 (1988): 127-34. doi:10.1016/s0899-3289(88)80016-6

Pacino, Al, Jack Lemmon, Alec Baldwin, James Foley, Jerry Tokofsky, and David

Mamet. *Glengarry Glen Ross*. Van Nuys, CA: Live Home Video, 1993.

Parker, Sarah Jessica, Lee Montgomery, Morgan Woodward, Shannen Doherty, and Helen Hunt. *Girls Just Wanna Have Fun*. 1985.

Pelzer, David J. *A Child Called 'It'*. Seven Dials, 2019.

Pychyl, T. A. *Fear of failure*. (2009) Psychology Today. https://www.psychologytoday.com/us/blog/dont-delay/200902/fear-failure.

Quick and Dirty Tips. Accessed on August 4, 2021. Quick and Dirty Tips ™

"The Harvard MBA Study on Goal Setting." *Quantum Books*, 24 July 2018, www.quantumbooks.com/home-and-family/personal-development/the-harvard-mba-study-on-goal-setting/.

Tseng, Julie, and Jordan Poppenk. "Brain Meta-State Transitions Demarcate Thoughts across Task Contexts Exposing the Mental Noise of Trait Neuroticism." *Nature News*, Nature Publishing Group, 13 July 2020, www.nature.com/articles/s41467-020-17255-9.

Made in the USA
Columbia, SC
11 September 2021